# Write Your Story

## How to Jump Start Your Writing Career

Stacey Ritz

*Write Your Story: How to Jump Start Your Writing Career*

Stacey Ritz.

Published by Rockville Publishing

Cover photograph credit iStock, Getty Images.

ISBN-13:978-1545190760

ISBN-10: 1545190763

PRINTED IN THE UNITED STATES OF AMERICA

# WRITE YOUR STORY

_____

*How to Jump Start Your Writing Career*

# Prologue

*"I am by nature a dealer in words, and words are the most powerful drug known to humanity."*

*-Rudyard Kipling*

You are a writer. Whether you're a published author, a journalist, a newsletter contributor or someone who quietly writes stories the world has yet to be given the privilege of reading, you are a writer. Put simply, if you write, you're a writer.

When someone asks me when I became a writer, I'm never quite sure how to answer. I marveled in wonder as I learned to read my first book. My veins filled with an unrelenting pulse when I held a pencil and paper in my young hands, consumed with the realization that I could write and create anything

I wanted with two tools. I've been enamored with books for as long as I can remember. My dad took me to used book stores when I wore pig-tails. My mom took us to the library religiously. My heart swelled standing in the company of so many unread books. I devoured every book I could get my hands on. *Some things never change.* I filled volumes of journals and notebooks with my own compilations of words. I wrote plays and urged my siblings and cousins to fulfill the acting roles for our reluctant audience of parents. I wrote stories in my notebook while riding on the bus to and from school. Living outside of town, I was the first kid picked up on the morning route and the last kid to step off the bus in the evening. I was a quiet bus rider, often sunk down in the seat with my nose buried in a book. I was so quiet that sometimes the bus driver forgot I was there, driving us both to her home only to realize she'd omitted me from her mind. This happened so often, eventually I began putting my book down as the last kids left the bus and waved my hands to remind Diane, the bus driver, that I was there too. Nevertheless, I had time, imagination, and my paper and pencil. I had everything I needed to create magic and that suited me just fine.

Fast forward several years and at age eighteen I

began mailing my manuscripts to New York City agents and publishers. I attended writer's workshops, entered writing contests and seized every opportunity I came across to write (for free) for newsletters and other publications. As the years rolled by, I began writing for several local newspapers. And then I wrote for a paper that paid me! I began blogging. I wrote for online news sources, sometimes earning up to $10 a month. That led to paid writing work for local magazines, and then national magazines. One experience led to another. Each one grew from the next. All the while, I continued reading obsessively, across a wide variety of genres. At this point I worked a full-time day job in an office and had co-founded and operated a non-profit organization for animals. Time was scarce, but I had to write. I made sacrifices such as giving up cable TV. I gave up eating out. I gave up my car. I wrote in the middle of the night while others slept. I wrote during my lunch hour. My bag was (and still is) full of a mess of notes written on napkins, receipts, gum wrappers, bank statements, pieces of cardboard, and scrap pieces of paper; each one scribbled with story ideas. I will write on anything. When I have a thought or an idea, I need to write it down quickly. I admit, I've even written my creative notes in the fog on the car windows, because it was the only viable place to write at the time. I've written those notes while sitting at red lights, while stuck in traffic jams and from beneath conference room tables as I sat in workplace meetings. I send text messages to myself, too. Do I sound ridiculous? Maybe I do, but hey, it's how I roll. It's who I am. I am a creative being who is bursting at the seams to put my thoughts on paper and when possible, to share those insights and stories with the world. It wasn't until I was just about to turn thirty-four that my first book published. When did I become a writer? In my heart, I've always been one. If you're here, I think it's safe to assume you write. Therefore, you are a writer. Maybe you're ready to publish your first book. Or maybe you have three published books, but they're not selling as well as you'd hoped. Wherever you are in your writing career, it's important to remember that each of us has a unique path. There is not a specific road map you must follow in order to reach your writing goals. If you're looking for a step-by-step guide of how to publish a book or how to get an agent, this is not it. In fact, I don't believe such a thing truly exists. You have to work hard, follow your passion and discover your own path. However, if you are looking for insights, motivation, and inspiration in your writing career, you've come to the right place. Whether you are (or are seeking to be) traditionally or indie (independently/self) published, you'll find this book a useful resource along your journey to jump starting your writing life. In *Write Your Story: How to Jump Start Your Writing Career* I'll share what I've learned (so far) along my journey and help you blaze your own trail as you work toward *your* goals. To date I have ten published books (and counting), in addition to many others which I've been a contributing writer. My books are both fiction and nonfiction. I've been a blogger, journalist, magazine writer, newsletter writer and more. My books and articles have won numerous awards and I have a bestselling book. I'm not sharing this information about myself to brag, rather, to let you know that you're in good company. We're in this together. We are all writers who want to write. We are writers who want to share our stories with the world. We are writers who want to make a positive impact in society. We are writers who struggle with self-doubt. We are writers who need to build a community. We are writers who need to market our books. We are writers who need to develop healthy habits to get us to our goals. We are writers who need to support each other, each traveling our own unique paths. We are writers who bravely let our hearts bleed on the page, allowing ourselves to be judged by the world. We are writers who are vulnerable. We are writers who fall victim to comparitinitus. We are writers who are human. We are people with dreams. We are people with loved ones and families. We are juggling jobs and holding onto those small moments of time when we can write. Above all, we are human. And we are writers. And we are in this together. Whether you dream of writing full-time, wish to publish a single book, or even if you're not sure specifically what your goal is just yet (you just know that you're a writer and you need to write), this book is for you.

- Do you love to write?

- Do you love to read?

- Do you love to tell stories?

- Do you love being creative?

- Do you love extra income?

- Do you want to be a published writer?

- Do you suffer from self-doubt?

- Are you fearful of criticism?

- Do you struggle with perfectionism?

- Do you compare yourself to other writers?

- Could you use a dose of motivation?

- Do you need to establish (or re-establish) healthy daily writing habits and practices?

If you answered yes to the questions above, keep reading. Remember, we're in this together. We're all writers and I'm here to help you along your unique journey to reach your writing goals.

> *"If you want to change the world, pick up your pen and write."*
>
> *-Martin Luther*

Persistence will get us where we want to go. Do you dream of holding a copy of your first published book in your hands? Do you hope to be a bestselling author? Do you want to sell 1,000 copies of your book? 10,000? A million? Do you wish to win the Pulitzer Prize? Whatever it is you want to do, persistence is your vehicle. Write every day. Read every day. Study your genre. Connect with other professionals in the writing field. And when the days are long and you're experiencing debilitating self-doubt, turn to writing. Whatever you do, if your dream is to be a writer, write. Just. Keep. Writing.

Writing is grueling. It's heart wrenching. To write is to reach deep into your soul and to sit with what you find. To examine life from every angle. To write is to live, but we must always remember to live if we are to write well.

Is writing easy? No. Nothing worthwhile ever is. But when we stain the pages of our writing with hard work, sweat, tears, and emotion, when we allow ourselves to be vulnerable to the page (and if it's a published work, to the world), it is worthwhile. Writing is an investment in ourselves and in the world. Words have the power to change the world. Ponder that for a moment. Words. The single tool we use to work our magic as writers, can produce change. For example, Harper Lee's *To Kill A Mockingbird* is credited with such a change. President Obama and the First Lady stated that Lee "changed America for the better. When Harper Lee sat down to write *To Kill a Mockingbird*, she wasn't seeking awards or fame. She was a country girl who just wanted to tell an honest story about life as she saw it…what that one story did, more powerfully than one hundred speeches possibly could, was change the way we saw each other, and then the way we saw ourselves... Through the uncorrupted eyes of a child, she showed us the beautiful complexity of our common humanity, and the importance of striving for justice in our own lives, our communities, and our country. Ms. Lee changed America for the better. And there is no higher tribute we can offer her than to keep telling this timeless American story- to our students, to our neighbors, and to our children- and to constantly try, in our own lives, to finally see each other."[1]

*Uncle Tom's Cabin* written by Harriett Beecher Stowe, a middle aged white woman in 1851 "has been credited for changing the views of slavery in the north and continues to serve as a reminder of the effects of slavery and other inhumane acts." While Anne Frank's *Diary of a Young Girl* "has become a symbol and reminder against racial persecution". And Henry David Thoreau's *Walden* "became a source of inspiration for those seeking a simpler more self-sufficient life."[2]

What books have inspired change in you? What books have altered your perception on a specific topic? Susan Cain's *Quiet* empowered me. I had spent years beating myself up for being different. After reading Cain's book, I realized that what I'd perceived as different was my introversion. Jodi Picoult's *Small*

*Great Things*, while disturbing and heartbreaking, is an important book on racism. Cheryl Strayed's *Tiny Beautiful Things: Advice on Love and Life from Dear Sugar* warmed my heart and reminded me that not only is it okay to be different, but we should celebrate our uniqueness. Stephen Madden's *Embrace the Suck* didn't necessarily change my world, but felt like a good friend standing by my side as I began my journey into the CrossFit world. Brene Brown's *Daring Greatly* pushed me forward on my life's journey to be more vulnerable and to let go of the idea of perfection. It's true, there are feel good stories and there are informative stories, but there are some stories that take hold of us by the shoulders, shake us to life and widen our eyes in a powerful way.

Words inspire change through the emotions they evoke. Words inspire change by the way they are strung together. What stories do *you* long to tell? From what perspective do you want to share your story? What emotions do you hope to awaken in your readers?

*"You should write because you love the shape of stories and sentences and the creation of different words on a page. Writing comes from reading, and reading is the finest teacher of how to write."*

Remind yourself every day that you are a writer. Remember, it doesn't matter where you are on your journey. We can only compare ourselves to the person we were yesterday. If you write, you are a writer. And you, dear friend, are a writer. Consider the following:

*One day...*

- You'll be someone's favorite author.

- A fan will ask you to sign their copy of your book.

- An aspiring writer will come to you for professional insight and guidance.

- You'll write a story that will change someone's life.

- You'll write a story that reminds someone they are not alone.

- You'll write a story that changes someone's perspective.

- You'll write a story that inspires someone to take action in an effort to make the world a better place.

- You'll attend your own author book

signing.

- Your book will help someone through a tough time.

- Someone will highlight a quote from your book.

- A reader will write down a quote from your book and hang it in their office as daily inspiration.

- You'll be a bestselling author.

- A fan will ask when your next book is coming out.

- A fan will contact you to tell you how much they appreciate your books.

*"Just write every day of your life. Read intensely. Then see what happens. Most of my friends who are put on that diet have very pleasant careers."*

*-Ray Bradbury*

How do you feel when you wake each morning? I know the obvious answer for most of us: tired. But go a little deeper. How do you *feel*? Do you feel excited for the day ahead? Do you feel dread? Do you look forward to the day you have scheduled?

I am going to assume that you love to write. And if you love to write, if you carve time out of your day, every single day, to write, you have something to look forward to. If you have a day job you dread, I totally get it. I know all too well how it feels to sit inside of your car, unable to make your legs walk from the parking garage to your workplace due to nothing more than utter dread. I know how it feels to be bored and unstimulated with your job. I know how it feels to be caged in a tiny cubicle, wondering if the walls really are closing in on you. I know how it feels to be in the wrong job. I've been there (more on this in my book, *Be Awesome: How to Live Your Best Life*). Nevertheless, if you are a writer and you make time to write every day, you have something to look forward to. You are doing something you love, even if it's only for thirty minutes each day. You have a creative outlet. You have a way to express yourself. You have discovered a mode for sharing your discoveries, insights and stories with others. You are building your craft. You are a life-long learner. You are a master observer of the world around you. You craft words into stories. Never forget that words and stories have the power to change the world.

Words have the power to heal. The power to motivate. The power to inspire action. The power to connect humanity. The power to connect the planet. Words, it seem, are made of magic. How amazing is it then that we get to work with something as powerful as magic?

*"Read a thousand books and your words will flow like a river."*

-*Virginia Woolf*

As I dug through my journals, old story notes, worn out notebooks filled with book ideas, outlines, manuscripts, rejection slips, and binders full of published articles, a stapled document slipped from one of the messy piles. The story was written on a typewriter, the edges of the dried liquid whiteout from decades ago, still visible. I couldn't help but smile at the memory of evenings spent with my dad's typewriter, the bottle of whiteout and a well-worn dictionary never leaving my side. The faded yellow Post-it that stuck to the front of the story shared my former teacher's thoughts, written neatly in cursive handwriting: "Poetic words!" It was feedback I'd been given on a story I'd submitted in a middle school Language Arts class. Why I'd kept that particular story amongst my myriad of publications and tired outlines, I have no idea. Perhaps it was a mistake. Then again, I may have held on to the story because of the Post-it note itself. Because of the feedback. I can't remember a time when I didn't want to be a writer and I have no doubt the Post-it filled me with hope all those years ago. *Maybe one day I really would be a writer*, I'd probably thought. Maybe one day I'll see my name on the front of a glossy book cover. And now, one day is here. Yet I still keep the story with the Post-it. I still stuff it back amongst my journals and binders, possibly as a reminder that someone believed in me. Possibly as a reminder that I became a writer many years ago. Or possibly as a reminder that words are charged with power. *Poetic words*, my teacher had written of my work. And although the statement is simple in nature, the two words remain meaningful to me. A teacher's words written long ago, hold the kind of meaning to me that I hope to instill in my readers- in *you*.

The Post-it motivated me to begin keeping a journal of positive feedback I receive from my published books. Whether it's a positive review left on any of the popular book reading websites or an email or letter sent to me telling me how one of my books helped someone, I hang on to those words.

Because there are days when I suffer from self-doubt. There are days when I read a mediocre or poor review and feel devastated. There are days when I sit down to write and fifty words later I've suddenly gone blank. And on those days, I can turn to my journal and read through some of the positive feedback and letters I've received over the years, and remind myself that what I'm doing matters. I encourage you to do the same. Keep your positive letters, emails and feedback in a safe place somewhere that you can access in these moments. If you've yet to publish an article or a book, hold on to your former teacher's words, as I did. Hold on to the encouraging words of your friends and family. It may sound silly, but hold on to positive self-talk, too. Believe in yourself. Tell yourself that you can and will reach your writing goals. With persistence, anything is possible. With a passion for what you do (writing), anything is possible. Just. Keep. Writing. Keep going. Keep working. Keep reading. Keep studying. And everything will fall into place. As you march along, forging your own unique path, hold on to the uplifting words that come your way. And always remember, *you* are a writer.

# 1

## Start Small

*"Good writers define reality: bad ones merely restate it."*

*-Edward Albee*

"Van Gogh created art whether anyone cared or not. He didn't need recognition or the applauding approval of an audience...he didn't need anyone to recognize his greatness. All he needed were his canvases, brushes, and paint."[1] As a writer, all you need is a pen and paper, or a computer and a flash drive. Do you find yourself writing what you're passionate about or what you think will sell? Do you seek approval from others or are you writing to tell a story or to dispense advice? Do you set small goals or do you have a habit of setting large goals and becoming frustrated when you don't get there quick enough?

Did you know bestselling author Seth Godin has received more than 900 rejection letters from book publishers? Stephen King had thirty rejections for his first novel, *Carrie*. It was because King's wife urged him to continue submitting the manuscript that the book was eventually published. John Grisham's first book, *A Time to Kill*, took three years to write and was rejected twenty-eight times before being published. J.K. Rowling, author of the Harry Potter fantasy series, was rejected by a dozen major publishers and was only published when, as reported on WiseBread.com "…a small London publisher chose to publish it only after the CEO's eight-year old daughter begged her father to print the book."[2] What do these writers have in common, apart from being bestselling authors? They set small goals along the way. They didn't sit down and say, I must be a bestselling author, or I will not write. Rather, they sat down and started writing. They sat down and shared a well-crafted story that was dying to be put on paper. They got to work. And they kept working. They continued writing, despite the self-doubt, despite the negative self-talk, despite the naysayers and the critics. They kept writing and it paid off.

Starting small means practicing your craft. It means writing stories that will likely never be read by the general public. It means writing articles and contributing to newsletters without pay. It means attending writer's workshops. It means reading constantly. It means writing every chance you get. It means blogging, joining a local writing group, volunteering to be a beta reader for a new author, writing for literary magazines, entering writing contests, submitting opinion editorials, writing book reviews. Starting small means you are ready to learn; you are ready for the journey.

Although I'd been writing my entire life, it was while hosting a fundraiser event for our non-profit organization that I met the editor of one of our local newspapers. I told him the story of how and why we founded our animal welfare organization and his eyes danced. "Do you happen to write?" He asked. I laughed and wondered why on earth this man had asked me such a question. At the time, I worked a full-time office/day job, operated the non-profit organization and I was running distance races competitively (which required regular training and traveling). When I nodded, he introduced himself and asked if I'd come downtown to the office to interview for a freelance position with the paper. Of course, I said yes. I didn't give any thought to when I'd find the time. I knew I would find it somewhere; after all, this was an opportunity to be paid to write! About the same time, I began writing for an online news source and a second local paper. Eventually that led to local and then national magazine work. Being paid for my writing was merely a bonus. When authors came to town on book tours, I was the first to volunteer to interview them and to write the book review. I loved learning how they got their start in writing. I felt inspired placing myself near published authors. And I soaked up every word they shared with me. Several years later, when I found myself on the other side of the table, I couldn't help but smile.

Every action we take is a building block. We are writers, so we must write. And as writers, we must seek and seize opportunities to better our craft. We must take small steps to keep moving forward. What small steps are you taking right now? Below are a few examples of small steps you can take to build to your writing life:

- Enter a writing contest

- Start a blog on a topic you're passionate about

- Be a guest blogger

- Submit an Op Ed for a local paper

- Become a freelance writer for a local paper

- Start or join a local writing group

- Start or join a local reading club

- Leave reviews online if you like a book (e.g., support other authors)

- Attend writing seminars and workshops

- Write every day (e.g., set a word count, "I will write 1000 words each day)

- Read every day

- Tell stories

- Write short stories

- Observe the world around you, take notes (i.e., future story ideas)

- Practice writing exercises (e.g., check out Melissa Donovan's books)

- Join a genre focused writing group or organization (e.g., Romance Writers of America)

- Volunteer to be a beta reader for other authors

- Submit article proposals to local and/or national magazines

- Contribute to a local non-profit newsletter

- Volunteer to help children learn to read/write

- Submit story proposals to literary magazines

- Participate in NaNoWriMo (nanowrimo.org)

- Join/participate in a non-profit writing organization (e.g., Women Writing for Change in Cincinnati, The Op Ed Project offered nationwide)

- Finish the book you're writing, even if you're experiencing self-doubt.

- Try writing a story outside of your genre

- Schedule a block of daily writing time (set a schedule)

What steps are you taking to empower your writing

career? What habits do you have that are holding you back? While it's important to dream and to have big goals, it's just as important to create small goals to get you there. Think of small goals as steps on a ladder. You need to take each step-in order to reach the top. In addition, each step will teach you something along the way.

While working for newspapers and magazines, I learned to work with editors. I learned *what* editors were looking for. I learned how to write compelling headlines and how to hook readers. I learned what topics were of interest to readers. I learned how to completely start an article over, even after thinking what I'd written was perfect. I learned to work with constructive criticism and when to defend my writing against over editing. I started to learn the sting of critical comments from random strangers. I learned that after publishing a cover story, there wasn't time to sit back and take in the fact that my name was on the front page. Rather, it was time to get to work and begin researching and writing the next article. And I learned that when you place yourself in an environment that you love, when you thrust yourself into the world of writing and surround yourself with other professionals in the field, you are laying a foundation for your career. You are stacking the building blocks of your writing life.

> *"I literally cannot remember a time when I did not want to be a writer."*

> *-J.K. Rowling*

I was terrified when I submitted my first article to the local paper. This was the first article I would ever be paid for and that meant something to me. I wanted it to be perfect (I hadn't yet realized that perfection does not exist). I wanted my article to be amazing. I wanted it to knock the publisher off his feet. I wanted to stand out. I wanted to be so stellar that someone would call me up the day after the article was published and offer me a book deal.

Unfortunately, reality didn't happen that way. Instead, I nervously submitted the article to the paper's editor and an hour later he sent it back with a note saying, "This is not the article we talked about. This is a story about a cat. Please resubmit." I was mortified. When I checked to be sure he was correct, my heart sank. Indeed, I'd mistakenly sent him a cat story; something I'd written for our non-profit newsletter. How could I have been so dumb? I scolded myself into oblivion before pulling it together and re-submitting the correct article with an apology for my mistake. My article published, I was paid, and continued to work for the paper, careful to never submit a random cat rescue story again (that is, until I wrote a commissioned piece on animal welfare). To be clear, I didn't receive a call from an agent after that first published newspaper article. I wasn't offered a book deal. Therefore, without a published book, I didn't become an overnight New York Times Bestseller. Bummer. Nevertheless, I continued writing, because I loved it.

Starting small not only creates opportunity to learn, it also allows us to grow at our own pace. And mistakes, unfortunately, will always be part of that journey. But mistakes give us yet another opportunity to learn. One writers journey is never an exact replica of another's. We are creatives and a creative life does not follow a specific agenda. A creative life does not say you must first do A and then move on to B…etc. A creative life, rather, allows us the freedom to discover our own steps. What works for one writer will not always work for another. Can we learn from each other? Certainly. We can always benefit from hearing each other's experiences. But can we follow an exact model to success? No way. To be clear, we all have different definitions of success.

To some, success is synonymous with fame. To others, success means financial freedom. Stop for a moment now and ask yourself, what does success mean to you? Be specific. To achieve success, what does that mean to you? What does it look like? What can you do to get there?

*"If you knew how much work went into it, you would not call it genius."*

*-Michelangelo*

Introduce yourself as a writer. The next time someone asks what you do for a living, tell them you're a writer. It will change your life. Don't believe me? Give it a try.

Why does introducing yourself as a writer change your life? Because you are admitting to yourself and to the world, what you are. You are making yourself accountable to your goal. By simply telling others that you're a writer, you solidify to yourself that you *really* are a writer. It's yet another form of positive self-talk; a small step that will send you forward. If you have yet to publish a book, you may feel reluctant to introduce yourself this way. If it's the follow-up question you are fearful of, "What books have you published"? Fear not. Share with them the title of the novel you're currently working on. Or share with them a blog, newsletter, newspaper or magazine you've contributed to. Remember, they're not asking what you've published to belittle you, in fact, it's often quite the opposite. They're asking what you've published because it gives them more insight into you and your interests. We grow when we push ourselves to expand. In my book, *Be Awesome: How to Live Your Best Life*, I pose the question: when was the last time you did something for the first time? Here is something small you can do for the first time. Introduce yourself as a writer. And no, you don't need to tag on "well, aspiring writer" or "I'm trying to be a writer." If you write, you're a writer. No need for add-on's or explanations. You are a writer and you should share your gift with the world.

I remember coming out of my own shell, telling people I was a writer when I first began writing for the newspaper. My stomach did flip-flops. Hearing myself say the words out loud began an internal transformation. I am a writer? I silently questioned myself as I stated to others that I was, indeed a writer. And then eventually my self-talk dropped the question mark and became, *I am a writer*. As this private shift took place within myself, additional writing opportunities started to appear. Do what you love, believe in yourself and an amazing revolution will ensue.

*"The secret to writing a bestseller: you write. You stop dreaming of writing. You stop talking about writing. Stop wishing you were writing. And you write."*

*-Jonathan Guneon*

What is your mission statement? To be a successful author in today's world you must be an entrepreneurial minded author. What is an entrepreneurial minded author? It's an author who understands that books are a business. The entrepreneurial minded author realizes that once you write the book, you must market it. As writers, many of us enjoy working in solitude, behind the comfort of our computer screens. However, once you write and publish your book, it's important to let readers know your book exists. Otherwise, how will anyone find your book? If our goal is to have a career in writing, you must treat your writing with respect and operate as the C.E.O. of your writing business. It is true, we are not really alone when we write. We work with a number of editors, publishers, beta readers, professional cover designers, and others. We are not in this alone. But it can often feel that way when we're in the heart of writing our novel, tucked away in our home office hunched over the computer, pounding out words that create a story.

Why do we need a mission statement? Because if we want to have a career in writing, we need to operate as a business, and businesses have mission statements. A mission statement is a short summary of the specific goals a company holds. While you can write a mission statement for your writing life as a whole, you may want to create a mission statement for each individual aspect of your writing life (e.g., blogs, books, articles). Or you may want to establish a mission statement for each book you write. Author Joanne Phillips[3] shared her mission statement, as follows:

*I write stories to entertain and offer a temporary escape into another life. I create interesting characters who may linger with the reader long after she's finished the story. I write about characters who learn to examine their lives – their motivations, their hopes and fears – and find the courage to change. I write about the important stuff, but with a light touch. I write about the four Ls: life, love, loss and lies – including the lies we tell ourselves. And yes, I want to change the world. A little tiny bit of it, anyway.*

Try writing a mission statement for your writing life, now. If you're working on a writing a book, next, write a mission statement specifically for your book.

*"Don't be 'a writer'. Be writing."*

*-William Faulkner*

Authors Sean Platt and Johnny B. Truant[4] know what they're talking about when it comes to writing. As creative entrepreneurs, they, along with a third partner, created the story studio, Sterling & Stone. They also operate the podcast network Sterling & Stone FM. In their book, *Iterate & Optimize*: *Optimize your Creative Business for Profit*, Platt and Truant share the small rules they live by in their own writing lives:

"We live by a few rules…

- Persistence is more important than perfection. If at first you don't succeed, it doesn't matter as long as you always try, try again.

- Small improvements, made consistently, add up.

- You cannot fail unless you quit. What most people call failures are merely unsuccessful experiments. Failures are bumps on the road as long as your story remains a work in progress.

- You can always do better with what you already have- and often, it's much smarter to find ways to do so than to invest time and money trying something entirely new as your next one sure thing.

- And most importantly, being good doesn't matter nearly as much as being slightly better than yesterday."

What rules do you want to live by in your own writing life?

Speaking of author entrepreneurship, mission statements, and rules to live by, let's not forget that by jump starting your writing life, you are catapulting yourself into a life that you love; to a life of work that you're proud of. Perhaps bestselling author Dale Partridge[5] said it best:

*"If you want something big in this life, find out how*

*to intensify your focus, multiply your motivation, and dig your heels deep into a life of discipline. You can't have a million dollar dream with a minimum wage work ethic. And you can't have a life you love without a lifetime payment of passion."*

Persistence itself is often viewed as a small thing. However, it is anything but. Ignoring the need for persistence in pursuit of your writing goals is to believe that there is a hidden easy button somewhere that no one is telling you about. There is no easy button to be found, and I'm sorry if I'm the first to break this to you. There just isn't. If you're still searching for a big green button that you can push to catapult you to all of your writing goals, you'll find the big green button is full of hard work, dedication and lots of time spent, you guessed it, writing. It's not do X and you'll achieve bestselling author status. It's a bunch of do A, B, C, D, E, F, G….and so on and take a calculated risk to see where that leads you. It's following this simple advice: just keep writing. If you're doing work that you love and that you believe in, even if it doesn't lead you to the exact dream you visualized at one point, it will lead you to good things. Surrounding yourself with the work you love (writing) will manifest people who also love that work and support your goal. It will manifest opportunities. Doors that you never imagined existed will suddenly begin to open. It most likely won't happen immediately, but it will happen with this small thing called persistence.

Don't underestimate the small things. Don't try and skip the small steps. They matter. And each experience, no matter how small, no matter unpaid or paid, no matter if it yields one reader or a million, each experience is a stepping stone forward. Don't be afraid to start small. Start by writing every day. Start by setting small goals. Start by telling the world that you're a writer (and by dropping the question mark when you say it to yourself. *I am a writer?* Upgrade that self-talk to: *I am a writer*). Be brave enough to take the first step to jump starting your writing life. Be bold enough to believe in yourself; to believe in your words. And be courageous enough to keep taking small steps; one after the other.

## 2

## Daily Practices

*"A professional writer is an amateur who didn't quit."*

*-Richard Bach*

### ESTABLISH A LONG-TERM GOAL FOR YOUR WRITING LIFE

What is your long-term goal in regard to your writing life? It's important to view your writing life through this lens. While jump starting your writing career is exciting, establishing your long-term goal is crucial to success. Whether you're just starting out as a writer or you've published several books, ask yourself, what is *your* long-term goal? For me, it has always been freedom. And while that term may mean different things to each of us, I have defined it for myself. And I remind myself of this goal in every action and decision I make. Once you define your long-term goal, it too, should play a big part in every decision you make in your writing life.

## PROFESSIONALISM

There are many things to consider when you're at the start of or revamping your writing career. Which programs will you utilize? Which professionals will you hire? There are a host of ever changing options for authors, publishers and marketers. From Vellum to Scrivener and beyond. I will not delve into specific program options nor recommend specific agents, editors or cover designers here, as this is an ever-changing market. Whether you're traditionally or indie (independently) published, it's important to realize you must hire a variety of professionals when publishing your book. Remember, you are the writer. If you want to be a professional at your craft, you need to focus on your writing and hire other professionals to focus on other aspects of your book (e.g., cover design, formatting). While it may seem that authors primarily work alone, that is not necessarily the case. Yes, we often do our writing alone. However, the research prior to our writing is often in collaboration with a host of others. Our constant need to continue learning is also a collaborative effort (e.g., writing groups, seminars). And after you've written your book, it's time again to work closely with other professionals such as a content editor, line editor, proofreader, copyeditor, book formatter, and cover designer, to name a few. I know what many of you are thinking: but I can do it all myself! While that may absolutely be the case, keep in mind that if you want to jump start your writing career, it's a non-negotiable to hire professionals to do what they do best, while you do what you do best- writing. If you want to put a well-polished, professional book into the world, working with professionals in their given field is an absolute must.

Do you have a friend who is willing to beta-read your book? That is terrific. However, that is not enough on its own to produce a professional product. While beta-readers can be incredibly helpful, a professional editor is necessary if you wish to have your work taken seriously. Do you want to edit the book yourself? You can and you absolutely should prior to handing it off to the professionals, but self-editing cannot compete with professional standards. The bottom line is, if you want to produce a professional product, you must operate as a professional and hire other professionals for those things that fall outside of your craft- writing.

As a bestselling author, every week I receive inquiries pleading, "How can I publish my book for free?" and "How can I market my book for free?" The questioners want me to either A) provide them with a one sentence answer or B) become their (free) personal publishing consultant. I can't do either of those. First, it's impossible to give a one sentence answer to such a big question. If I must provide an answer in a few short sentences, I say: "Becoming an author requires an ongoing investment in learning not only the craft of writing, but also in a myriad of other aspects such as hiring editors, professional book formatters and cover designers, etc. It is incredibly hard work." As for the *free* part of the questions above: nothing worthwhile is ever easy (aka: free). You must give your time; a lot of it. You must work with professionals. Another question I receive daily is, "How much does it cost to self-publish my book?" Again, there isn't one specific answer to this question. We each have our own unique path. Cost will depend on you. What is your long term goal? What are your short term goals? Editors vary in cost. Book cover designers vary in cost. Professional formatting for both print and e-books vary in cost. Costs vary between hardback, paperback, eBooks, audiobooks, etc. There is not a one-size (or in this matter, price) fits all answer. Everything depends on the choices you make as the entrepreneur of your writing life. Wait a minute, entrepreneur? Yes. Regardless of how you publish, you are the entrepreneur of your writing life. You are in the driver's seat. You make the decisions. And as with any business, when you are the owner, you have to figure out your path as you go. Set goals, create a map to get there, but be flexible along the way. When we work toward our goals, we learn, adapt, modify and grow. As for the marketing question (above), we'll delve more into that topic in Chapter 9. There are options to capitalize on free marketing endeavors, but again, while they may be free monetarily, they cost in terms of your time, energy and efforts. More on that later.

Another important consideration authors must make: do you want to self-publish a book to see your name in print (with no concern about selling to others)? Or do you want to sell your books and make an income through writing? They are two very different things and answering this question while you are jump starting your writing life, is a must. It's important to note, except for the occasional break-out star, you cannot publish one book and expect fame, stardom and piles of money. In fact, if you're writing for any of these reasons, I urge you to stop immediately. Writers should strive to publish a book when they have a story to tell or helpful information to share. While we can all agree that extra income is always welcome, if your dream is to publish a book solely for the purpose of fame and wealth, you likely will not have a long-term career in the field.

Did you know, most writers stop publishing after just two or three books? However, readers trust authors with large backlists. The more books you have (especially when they all concentrate on a particular topic), the more likely a new reader is to give your book a chance. We are living in a day and age of binging. We crave rainy weekends full of Netflix binges or reading a book series. We want to know that we'll enjoy the stories we are watching/reading/listening (audiobooks) to. We want to feel that we know the characters. Surveys show that readers remember an author's name more often than they will remember a book title. Therefore, it is imperative to brand yourself. Let yourself be known for a specific genre, or a specific topic. If you write nonfiction, write about what you're already an expert in and enthusiastic about. Readers want to learn and we want to learn from experts who are (and who demonstrate that they are) experienced and knowledgeable in their field. When writing and marketing your book, always consider the reader. *If you're a writer, you should be a reader.* And as a reader, you know what you want. You know what book covers catch your eye and why. You know which hooks keep you reading a novel. You know that you'd rather read a "how to" book written by not only a demonstrated experienced expert in that field, but also someone who is likeable and relatable. Apply these little wisdoms to your own author business and writing life. If you fail to do so, you are selling yourself short. You will miss out on readers if you never consider what your readers want.

Other considerations to make while jump starting your writing career: will you publish traditionally or independently? Will you work with an agent? Where will you find trustworthy beta-readers? Have you spent time researching editors? Who will you hire? Will you work with a big publisher or a small press? If you're self-publishing, where will you publish? Will your book be available in paperback? eBook? Audiobook? Hardback? Furthermore, what is your niche? Nonfiction or fiction? Short stories, novellas, or novels? Genre? Does your writing fall in a cross-genre? Who is your intended audience? Will you write under a pen name? Will you write with a co-author? If writing nonfiction, are you an expert in your field? How will readers find your books? Do you have a website? Blog? Social media? Marketing budget? What writing seminars and workshops will you attend this year?

Earlier I mentioned the importance of operating your writing life as a business. Remember, you are the entrepreneur of your writing life. You need short term and long-term goals. You need a mission statement for your writing life. Create a mission statement for each new book, too. Define your genre/niche. Write a business plan for your writing career. It may feel silly at first, but it is your map; your guide. What else do business owners do? They work hard. They plan. They put in the time. They collaborate with other professionals. They strive to put a professional product into the world. And if they love what they do, it shows. If you're a writer, write. Write, not to get rich or to be noticed, but because you have to. Write because you love it. Write because it's who you are. Write because you have a story to tell.

*"Better to write for yourself and have no public, than write for the public and have no self."*

*-Cyril Connolly*

## PRIORITIZE WRITING AND READING TIME

Are you willing to prioritize your writing and reading time? Many aspiring writers contact me and tell me they dream of becoming a published author, but they just don't have the time. If you can relate, consider the following: beloved author J.K. Rowling had the idea for Harry Potter while sitting on a delayed train. She wrote the idea on a napkin. Author Claire Cook wrote her first book in a minivan, at age 45. Her website bio shares, "At 50, she walked the red carpet at the Hollywood premiere of the romantic comedy movie adaptation of her second novel, *Must Love Dogs*, starring Diane Lane and John Cusack. She is now the *New York Times*, *USA Today* bestselling author of 17 books and a sought-after reinvention speaker."

I began submitting my books to publishers when I

was a full-time college student, an NCAA athlete and working over summer breaks. I continued writing and submitting books to publishers when I was working 12-hour days (with a one-hour commute each way, if traffic cooperated), while operating a growing non-profit organization, and writing for two local newspapers, when my first book published. Writing must be a priority. Writing a novel (and writing as a career) is a marathon, not a sprint. Pace yourself and work at your craft every single day. Carve out designated time to write each day, whether that be at a desk, in a café, sitting in a minivan or some other creative spot. Here are a few ideas to help you get started (i.e., how to find time to write):

- Write on your commute to/from work
- Write during your lunch hour
- Wake up early and write before work
- Stay up an hour later and write each night before bed
- Write on the weekends
- Write while you're waiting for your child to take a class (e.g., gymnastics)

What are you willing to give up to be a writer? Time is an obvious one. Outside of that, what comforts are you willing to exchange to spend quality time writing? Will you cut cable television and opt to spend more time reading? Will you stop eating out to save both time and money (which can be then utilized toward your writing life)? Will you stop taking vacations while you work on writing your first ten novels? Will you give up your vehicle? These are a few of the sacrifices I made for my writing life. Every choice we make in life has a consequence. And I chose to give up luxuries such as these, to lessen my financial burden and to provide myself with more time to focus on writing.

If you want to be a writer, you must make time to write. Turn off your phone. Turn off the television. Turn off social media. We are surrounded by temptations. To write well, however, we need to focus. And while focus can come in any environment (e.g., in a minivan or in the workplace cafeteria), we need to find the discipline to do it.

Outside of writing, the number one thing writers can do to hone our craft, is to read. Read everything you can. Cereal boxes. Books by a wide variety of both indie and traditionally published authors. Short stories. Novellas. Billboards. Read books in a wide variety of genres (don't limit yourself). Read newspaper articles. Read blogs. Read fiction and nonfiction, regardless of what you personally write. Everything you read will help add another building block to your writing life.

Are you submersing yourself into the world of writing? Submersing yourself into this world means writing and reading books every day. It means that you don't only talk about writing, but that you are writing. What writing books have you read? A few of my favorites are: *Write. Publish. Repeat.* (Sean Platt and Johnny B. Truant), *The Artists Way* (Julie Cameron), *The Writing Life* (Anne Dillard), *Wired for Story: The Writer's Guide to Using Brain Science to Hook Readers From The Very First Sentence* (Lisa Cron), *The Best American Short Stories* (Junot Diaz). *Still Writing: The Perils and Pleasures of a Creative Life* (Dani Shapiro), and *Do the Work* (Stephen Pressfield). I'm a reading fanatic; I could go on and on. But I'll stop there. You'll gather your own basket of favorites as you delve into your extensive reading on writing.

## OUTSIDE OF WRITING

Are you an observer of life? Do you find yourself collecting conversations and interactions that you witness (for future story inserts)? Utilize the power of survey with your readers. Ask them. What is it they are dying to know about your topic of expertise? It's possible you already know. This book, after all, is based on the top questions I'm asked week after week about writing, publishing and marketing. If you write fiction, poll your readers (or if you don't have readers yet, poll those who read in the genre you wish to write). Ask what keeps them hooked in a story. What are their favorite books? Take their feedback seriously and read the books they state as their favorites. Learn why they like the books they do. How do their favorite authors hook the reader from the first sentence? How do they keep the reader interested throughout the story? Begin reading books as a writer. Reading books like a writer means reading, not solely for pleasure, but with thought. Reading like a writer means that you are reading to study the clues, to learn from the masters.

While you are studying other books in your genre, check out the reviews. You can learn a lot from reading both the five star and one star reviews. What can you learn from a one star review? Actually, quite a lot. You can learn what disappointed the readers.

What were they hoping for that they feel the author didn't deliver? Will you be able to provide this detail in your own story? When reviewing five star reviews, seek to find specifically what the readers enjoyed. Was it the pacing of the book that stood out to them? Did they mention that the cover is why they purchased the book? Or perhaps they love the author because he/she has a huge back list and they're working on reading all of their books. Study and learn. There are countless lessons we can absorb from the professionals while jump starting our own writing life.

While writing daily is an important part of being a writer, ask yourself, do you spend time visualizing the act of achieving your writing goals (goals outside of fame and money)? Do you believe in yourself? How is your self-talk? Positive self-talk goes a long way. It costs nothing to make this switch. Positive self-talk is free and available to everyone, every day. You may be wondering if it really matters how you talk to yourself. Consider this: positive self-talk can transform outcomes. Positive self-talk is powerful. Of course, positive self-talk on its own won't get you to all your goals, however, when paired with consistent hard work, it will. "The brain will believe whatever you tell it most." Shares Sound-Mind.org.[1]

"Therefore, you must spend time each day repeating new, positive self-talk to yourself. It is only through repetition that your brain will adopt its new reprogramming." It's easy to fall into the habit of negative self-talk; scolding yourself when a magazine doesn't pick up the article you worked hard on, or telling yourself you'll never make it as a writer whenever you miss a day of writing. Equally as hard of a habit to break is falling into the "I'll be happy when…" pitfall. This is when you tell yourself, "I'll be happy when I sell my first 1,000 books." Or "I'll be happy when I have 25 five-star online reviews." We don't have to wait to be happy. We can be happy right now when we focus on what we *do* have; when we focus on gratitude. Next time you catch yourself thinking, "I'll be happy when…" change it to "I'm happy now because…" While achieving goals is exhilarating, working toward them should be celebrated, too. As for the self-talk, start paying attention to what you're telling yourself each day. It can be helpful to track your self-talk for two full-days. Write down each time you catch yourself thinking of yourself in a particular way. Is your self-talk more negative or positive? What can you do to improve upon it?

Do you understand your own worth? You are a

creative being. You are a writer! You have the ability to bring captivating stories to the world. You have the ability to teach us what you've become an expert in. You are capable of vulnerability. You are courageous. You are a professional. You are enough exactly as you are. Now, believe it.

Do you surround yourself with people who support you and your writing goals? If you have one person in your corner, count yourself as lucky. One person can make all the difference in our belief in ourselves, and in our eventual success. We don't have to have another person believe in us to succeed, but it certainly helps. Find friends, family members, co-workers, neighbors and others who motivate you. If they offer to be a beta-reader for a magazine article or novella, even better! By surrounding ourselves with those who lift our spirits, we can impact our future. "One of the most important decisions we make in life is who we choose to be around. In fact, there is an old proverb that reads, *'Show me your friends and I'll tell you who you are.'* Quite often we become like the people we're around. Based on that, we must be cautious about whom we surround ourselves with because of the short and long-term implications," writes Clint Swindill for Forbes.[2] For example, if you spend a lot of time with people who complain about their jobs, likely you will begin complaining about yours too (and focusing on anything negative in your life). If you surround yourself with those lacking goals or motivation, it can rub off on you. Of course we're all prone to moments of self-doubt and negativity, but the analysis of who we surround ourselves with the majority of the time is based on the norm. When you spend time with your friends, do you typically leave feeling more energized or feeling lousy? This alone can tell you a lot. Does your support system of friends both support and challenge you? It makes sense then, if you are (or want to be) a successful entrepreneur (of your writing life), surround yourself with successful entrepreneurs, creatives and writers. If you don't know any of these people yet, don't worry. You will if you continue on your path to jump starting your writing career. If you stay dedicated to your writing goals and the creation of your writing life, you will make new contacts as you grow. And in the meantime, surround yourself with those who support you (and whom you support). Surround yourself with books. Lots of books, and lots of great authors. Surround yourself with writing podcasts, articles, blogs, seminars, and workshops. Swindill adds, Some "…people in our lives [who] drain us of our energy because they thrive on sharing their own negativity. Refuse it. Don't just walk away from the negativity–run. Get as far away from it as you can. Not only does it impact our perspective with regard to our own lives, it impacts our mental health. While your success can be determined in part by whom you surround yourself with, it can also be determined in part by whom you choose to not surround yourself with."

Do you empower others to reach their goals? This goes hand-in-hand with surrounding ourselves with supportive people. Be a team player. After all, it's much more fun to cheer for each other than to try and tear each other down. There is more than enough magic in the world for everyone to be successful. Author Brené Brown writes, "Stay in your own lane. Comparison kills creativity and joy." Don't fall prey to comparitinitis. It's not about being better than anyone else. Rather, strive to be better than the person you were yesterday. If you meet with a local monthly writing group and a member named Jim, excited about the publication of his first book, brings a hardback copy to show the group, don't hang your head because he published a book before you. Celebrate in Jim's victory. Learn from his journey. And keep writing every day. Keep being the C.E.O. of your writing life. Keep focused on *your* long-term goals. And keep believing in yourself. Remember, there is plenty of room for everyone to succeed. We're all on a unique path in our creative endeavors.

The brain doesn't know the difference between what we visualize and what is actually happening. In other words, when we visualize something specific, the brain believes it is actually occurring. This explains why those who experience P.T.S.D. often suffer from ensuing panic attacks. When a rape survivor suffers a flash back three years after the trauma occurred, her brain believes the attack is happening all over again. At the movie theater, have you ever noticed, when a tense scene is playing on the big screen, often viewers will wrap their arms around themselves in a protective measure? This is because, again, the brain believes what we are watching on the screen is actually occurring to us. And if this is true, it must mean that what we visualize (hence, the importance of positive self-talk), we believe. Visualize yourself taking specific steps to becoming a *New York Times Bestselling* author. Visualize your name on your beautiful, professional book cover with the tagline of "Bestselling Author" written at the top. Visualize what you wish for yourself. It may sound crazy, but it also just might come true. Positive affirmations and meditation are a few ways to improve your visualization practice.

The Law of Attraction is responsible for bringing both positive and negative influences into our lives. Widely publicized by *The Secret* (Rhonda Byrne), the Law of Attraction is the ability to bring into our lives, what we focus on. While you can create a vision board for this purpose, the Law of Attraction goes beyond the board. An attitude of gratitude (i.e., focusing on what we are grateful for and what is good in our lives) can bring an abundance of more good to our lives. What does this have to do with writing? A lot, actually. We can utilize the Law of Attraction in our writing lives to grow and create additional opportunities. For example, you had magazine articles published during the last quarter, but you haven't published your first book. In fact, you haven't been able to finish writing the novel you've been working on for two years. Rather than focusing on what you haven't yet accomplished, focus on what you have. Celebrate every victory. Every article you publish is teaching you something about yourself and your writing. What do readers respond to? How do you hold a reader's interest? What headlines do you find more impactful (and how can you translate that to your future book titles)? Don't forget the fact that you are a published writer. So, you're not an author yet. *You will be.* Keep writing. Keep visualizing. Keep reading. Keep focusing on your goals. You'll get there. We have a choice every day. We have a choice every moment, every decision. How will we choose to view the situation? How will we choose our inner dialogue? What will we focus on? Use the Law of Attraction to your advantage as you jump start your writing career.

## MAKE SMART MOVES

The focus of this chapter is on both creating healthy daily writing habits and considerations to make while enhancing your writing life. This should go without saying, but just in case you're not doing this, *always* back up your work. Whether you're typing a blog or you're in the middle of writing your fifth novel, back-up your work. Early on, in my own writing career, I neglected to follow this simple rule. When my computer decided to have a mind of its own, I lost the cover story I'd just finished researching and writing. I lost the blog content I'd pre-written for the upcoming month. There was no way to retrieve the content. I had to start from scratch and type the content again. I spent hours of my time re-doing work I'd already done because I'd failed to back-up my work. We put a lot of time and effort into our writing, the least we can do is make sure we don't lose it.

Don't give up your day job too soon. Bestselling author and financial guru Suze Orman encourages everyone (not only writers) to, at minimum, have at least a six-month emergency fund saved. Thriller author J.F. Penn advises not only to have an emergency fund, but to also have a regular income of at least $1000 a month with a backlist of books and other sources of income (preferably with the $1000 per month coming from your book sales) before saying good-bye to your day job and leaping into writing full-time. Too often, writers believe they'll publish a novel and immediately quit their day job. And too often, those same writers are deeply disappointed. As a side note, if you receive an advance on your first book, remember, the advance may need to be paid back (at minimum, the publisher will not begin paying you until they have recouped the advance). If you are receiving royalties, keep in mind not only can this amount change, book sales will fluctuate from month to month, and without a marketing budget, book sales may, in fact tank. To break it down further: [the advance] is "paid against future royalty earnings, which means that for every dollar you receive in an advance, you must earn a dollar from book sales before you start receiving any additional royalty payments. So, for example, if I were to receive a $10,000 advance with a royalty rate that works out to $1 per book sold (royalties are measured in percentages, but for the sake of this explanation let's keep it simple), you would have to sell 10,000 books to pay off your advance. If your royalty rate worked out to $5 a book, you'd have to sell 2,000 copies. And so forth. After the publisher recoups your advance, it will begin to pay you royalties on subsequent sales based on the percentages outlined in the contract" explains Brian Klems.[3]

The bottom line is, build your niche while building a hefty backlist. Realize that marketing your book is an ongoing process, if you want to continue having sales. And don't quit your day job until you've saved an adequate emergency fund and you're bringing in a steady stream of income from book sales each month for an extended period of time. It's easy to get excited and want to make the leap too soon, but don't forget your long-term goals. Hopefully, you are writing for the long-haul (and not to make a few extra bucks overnight). Building a writing career is similar to building a brick house. First, we must choose our site (genre/niche). Then we must lay the foundation (submerse ourselves in the world of writing and write every day). Then we can begin stacking the bricks, one at a time (submitting our work for publication; articles, blogs, and eventually books). One thing must come before the other. If we rush ahead and forget about laying the foundation, we may be able to stack a few bricks and feel proud that we've skipped a big step in the process. But we're stacking the bricks on uneven ground and eventually, when the wind blows, the bricks will collapse. Cultivating our best writing life requires time, dedication, hard work, and lots of patience.

Another smart move we can make when jump starting our writing career is to diversify. As the entrepreneur and C.E.O. of our writing business, we are investing in ourselves. If you invest your money in the financial market, you can optimize your return by diversifying where you invest your money. We want to spread the risk. We don't want to have all of our eggs (or books!) in one basket with one retailer. Rather, we want to have our books available everywhere, to reach the most readers possible. Diversifying our books means creating a scalable income for ourselves. What is a scalable income? It is when we create something that can be sold over and over again, without rebuilding that product for each and every customer (e.g., books, especially eBooks fit well here). When we publish a book, we can not only sell that book across a wide number of markets, but we can also create multiple products from one book. Our book can be published as a paperback, hardback, ebook and audiobook. In addition, we can create content marketing in the form of T-shirts, mugs, journals, workbooks, and other products that play off of our book. This creates multiple streams of income from one product. Diversifying our books in these manners creates scalable income and allows us to reach a wider audience. Author Joanna Penn blogged, "Yes, we write because we love it and we feel a compulsion to create. But in a world where what was previously considered an asset may turn out to be false hope. A book is something that will last and may continue to earn money in your lifetime even after your death. I know your writing journey may be different from mine, but I am now a full-time author-entrepreneur and I need to make money from my writing. Yes, I love the writing and the process but I also need to make it work professionally." Penn added: "Yesterday, I returned home to a 4-figure check for the sales of my eBooks from February. My physical property never left me with that much per month."[4]

Speaking of investing, another consideration to make that will impact your writing life is to invest in yourself as a life-long learner and as a professional writer. This means setting aside funds to attend writing retreats and workshops each year. This means buying and reading (library cards help with this expense!) a lot of books from a lot of different authors in a lot of different genres. Investing in your writing life means setting aside time to write every single day. It means connecting with other writers. Connecting with your readers. Working with other professionals (e.g., editors, book cover designers). Investing in your writing means taking yourself seriously and believing in your work. It means *doing* the work. It means not only calling yourself a writer, but spending large amounts of time writing.

As writers, we know that some days the words flow onto the page seamlessly. We type 4,000 words and feel satisfied and accomplished at the end of the day. We achieved a quality writing session. Other days, writers block can smack us across the face, rendering us blank. We stare into oblivion hoping words will find us, only to find our minds wandering off to random topics (such as when will the next episode of

*This is Us* be on Hulu)? The world often fantasizes the life of a writer, picturing the lone writer sitting behind her computer, derrière resting in a porch rocking chair as she feels the salty air of the ocean breeze across her face. She begins writing at sunrise with a warm cup of coffee beside her and not a worry in the world to trouble her. She takes a long lunch and follows it up with a nap, only to return to her outdoor set up and write again in the afternoon. As the sun sets she sits back and smiles and realizes she's written a quarter of her novel in a short day's time. She then checks her bank account and sees that the money is pouring in. This, is what many picture the life of a writer to be. One of the questions I'm most often asked is "How can I be a writer?" When my answer runs longer than a short sentence, the questioner's eyes glaze over. They don't want to hear that it's hard work. They don't want to hear that it takes years (as it does with any business you begin) to make a profit. They don't want to hear that you must lay the foundation before you stack the bricks. And they don't want to hear that writing (whether you write articles, blogs or books) is done to start a conversation, not to chase fame and fortune. They want the fantasy, not the reality. The reality of the writing life, as with anything worthwhile, is that it is long, hard work. The reality is when you're creating your writing life, a life you love, you are likely to be working when others are not. And the reality is, the life of a writer is not usually glamorous. It most certainly can be one day, if that's what your goal is, but often, the best writers are writing because they want to start a conversation. Because they want to professionally exercise their creativity. Because they want to work magic with words. Because they want to make an honest difference in the world. The reality is, even when you love your writing life, hard work is sometimes boring. It's not to say you're not passionate about your writing, only that when you're working to achieve a goal it is about doing the work. As professionals, as writers, we know that doing the work is necessary. Doing the work, writing every day, investing in your writing life, is what makes you great. It's what builds success. It's what teaches us to be better at our craft.

With so much hard work, how do we avoid burnout with our writing? We want to avoid burnout so that our writing stays fresh and we stay inspired. How do we do this? We pace ourselves. As we're jump starting our writing career, we need to remind ourselves we're in this for the long haul. We are writers, after all. And if we're in it for the long haul, that means we want to keep writing. We want to keep publishing articles, blogs, and books. We want to, at the very least, incorporate writing into our daily life. Regardless of where you are in your writing career, burn-out can strike at any time and it is very real. Burn-out occurs when we overwork ourselves. When we're overwhelmed with our writing workload and/or the juggling of our many responsibilities in life. Burn-out occurs when we've pushed too hard. When we're spreading ourselves too thin, for too long. Pace cannot be emphasized enough. Healthy daily habits (many of which we've discussed throughout this chapter) can keep us well paced. Setting realistic short- and long-term goals can also help us in this endeavor. Celebrating the small victories can prove beneficial, too. Between books or when we feel run down, we need to practice self-care.

Taped to a cabinet in my office is a quote I pulled from an old calendar years ago that reads:

*"Don't forget to glance up from your keyboard and see how blue the sky is now and then. Don't forget to put away your cell phone and spend some time alone with paintbrush or pen. Don't forget to seek the sound of silence and let the daily traffic rush on by. Remember*

*that the secret of success is how happily you climb and not how high."*

And it was Albert Einstein who said, "I think ninety-nine times and find nothing. I stop thinking, swim in silence, and the truth comes to me." Take a mid-day break to walk outside. Or walk in the morning and the evening, before and after work. Exercise in any form is beneficial for our physical and mental state of being. Going for a walk outdoors can get you out of your head. Stepping away from the computer and taking in the fresh air can renew your energy. Walking, or any form of exercise will enhance not only your daily life as a writer, but will serve to help you reach your long-term goals. Daily walks can help you reach your long-term writing goals by preventing burn-out. While taking breaks may seem counterproductive, it's actually quite the opposite. Author Murray Newlands wrote, "...Stanford recently conducted a survey that concludes that daily walks improve productivity and creativity..."in his article titled, *How Two 15-Minute Walks Daily During Work Has Increased Company Productivity by 30%.*[5] He added, "...I decided to put this idea to the test. For 30 days, we asked that everyone (if physically able) in our office take two 15-minutes "walkies" (aka 15-minute walks) per day — no phones allowed. The result was a quantifiable jump in productivity of 30 percent." Newlands argues that short walks during the work day are helpful for several reasons including: boosting work satisfaction, improving focus and attention. In addition, University of Illinois at Urbana-Champaign researchers found, *"…stepping away and going on a walk provides different sights, sounds, and feelings that re-energize the brain. When we return to our desks, what we see and experience feels new again, so attention and productivity increase."* Mid-day walks allow our mind time to rest and re-charge, and we can combat burn-out and depression.

# 3

# Writing is a Marathon

*"If I waited for perfection, I would never write."*

*-Margaret Atwood*

Writing is similar to a marathon. A full marathon is 26.2 miles (42 Kilometers). You can't go out and run a marathon without prior training. If you try, you're setting yourself up for disaster. Just as you can't write a book without having created a solid foundation (i.e., years of practice, writing courses, seminars, workshops, reading books, publishing articles, etc.). The little things, repeated over time, add up. And even after dedicated training for a marathon, the race itself still boasts a big challenge. Neither running a marathon, nor writing a novel (or writing as a long-term career) is for the faint of heart. Although preparation is essential, no matter how much we train leading up to the actual marathon, there are never any guarantees. We know that we'll have an experience, but what that journey will yield, we have no way of predicting. We must put in the hard work, day after day, mile after mile, and do our best. In my experience, here is what running a marathon can teach us about our writing life:

## TRAINING IS A MUST

We must build a foundation for ourselves so that we do not set ourselves up for injury. If we want to succeed (finish the marathon/finish the novel), we must put in the work. The last marathon I ran was in Houston, Texas. I flew there, in an attempt to run a qualifying time for the Olympic Marathon Trials. I'd been training and racing long-distance for nearly a decade. I was a Division-I NCAA All-American Cross-Country runner in college. Following college, I traveled and raced competitively throughout the mid-west, winning prize money and racing under several small company sponsorships. I'd run one previous marathon, several half-marathons and countless miles on sidewalks, roads, trails, and treadmills. I was ready. Or so I'd thought. I had spent years laying the foundation and stacking bricks. I had spent ample time dreaming of this moment and what might come next. However, I left the race disappointed and embarrassed. I went out too fast and suffered later in the race. I did not run a qualifying time and could hardly shuffle my feet, one in front of the other, to get to the finish line. To add to the devastation of the day, I'd thought by qualifying to The Olympic Trials, I'd be able to leave my mundane office day-job and run full-time (with an increase in sponsorships). Falling short of the qualifying time left me lingering in a deep depression. I felt trapped in an office-job that bored me to tears. I'd spent so many years training for this moment. The next Olympics wouldn't arrive for four more years and I wasn't sure I wanted to continue training at the same level of intensity any longer.

Although this story seems to have a terrible, uninspiring ending, it doesn't. It's true, I metaphorically had the wind knocked out of me upon the completion of this marathon. I wasn't sure what move to make next. I wasn't even sure if I wanted to continue racing and competing. All the while, I quietly continued writing. And just two short years later, I landed my first paid writing gig. While training (building a foundation in our writing) is a must, there are never any guarantees. A creative life doesn't protect us from the pitfalls of life's ups and downs, rather, it takes us on a journey. On that journey we will be knocked down- in training and during the race. It will happen. We can't control it. But what we can control is how we react. When we get knocked down, we can decide to stay on the ground and sob, or to get back up and keep going. After the Houston marathon, my ego was admittedly bruised, but I stood back up and I kept going. I kept writing. Although I took some time off to recover, I also kept running (although my running grew to take on a new purpose and meaning). I kept doing the things I loved. I realized then, although I had a foundation, I needed to stack more bricks. We're never done stacking our bricks. We're never done building. When we choose to live a creative life, we are always inventing, creating, expanding, and experimenting.

## SET REALISTIC GOALS

If you're running your first marathon, your goals are likely to be different than someone who is racing their fifteenth. As writers, we need to set realistic goals for ourselves, too. Setting realistic goals allows us to enjoy the journey. When we love what we're doing, while goals are important, it's the path we carve out for ourselves to get us to our intended destination that allows us to grow and learn. Setting realistic goals will also prevent burnout.

*Side note:* If you dedicate yourself to writing 1000 words a day for just 60 days, you can write an entire novel! If you're more comfortable with 500 words a day, it's possible you can write your novel in 4 months.

## WHEN YOU GET KNOCKED DOWN, STAND BACK UP

We have a choice. Every moment. Every interaction. Every morning. Every hour. We always have a choice. When we get knocked down, we can stay there and weep or we can stand back up and keep moving forward. We have a choice every day to write or not to write. We have a choice to find pockets of time to read or to watch television. We have a choice to believe in ourselves or to fall victim to self-doubt. Life is full of choices. We choose to be in a good or bad mood. We choose to be helpful or hateful. The point is, we make choices. And every choice has a consequence (whether positive or negative). When we get knocked down, we have a choice to stand back up.

A runner who fell at the end of her distance race began crawling toward the finish line, unable to pull herself to a standing position. The fall rendered her injured, yet she'd run so many miles, it was important to her to cross the finish line. This is a race, mind you. Everyone is competing against themselves (to finish the race), but many are also competing for various time and placement goals. Dozens of runners ran past the crawling athlete, focused on their own finish line. But then, a runner stopped, undoubtedly slowing her own time and placement. She asked the crawling athlete if she was okay and then offered her own shoulders as a crutch. She pulled the ailing runner from the ground, hoisted her in the air and walked to the finish line, carrying the stranger in her arms.

Neither runner planned on finishing the race in such dramatic fashion. However, both runners took what came their way and made the best of it. Because of this, they both left the race feeling proud. In our writing lives we can do the same. Work hard, train and prepare, and if you can help a fellow writer along the way (e.g., advice, mentorship), do so. When you get knocked down, stand back up. And if you stumble across another writer who's been knocked down, provide encouragement.

## MAKE HUMAN-CONNECTION

When we can emotionally connect to other human-beings, we all succeed. In writing, human-connection is essential. It is, after all, the reason we read. We long to learn about and from those connections, even when they're not our own.

Just as the two runners made a connection at the end of the marathon (in the story above), we need to make the same type of connection with our readers. It must be authentic in nature, and we (the readers) must have a reason to care about why this connection matters. Our experiences are thoroughly enriched when we can connect with each other.

## DON'T FEAR OBSTACLES, OVERCOME THEM

Obstacles, much like setbacks (e.g., falling down) are inevitable in our writing life. It's how we choose to react to those obstacles that defines us. Whether you have a tight deadline or you're in a disagreement with your editor, obstacles happen.

During my first marathon, I ran through the streets of Kentucky with eight toenails. Two had painfully gone missing during the course of my training; lost to chronic blisters. I could have decided not to run the marathon, but my years of training taught me that missing toenails were part of the long distance running experience. I'd learned how to properly care for them and I'd found a professional podiatrist to whom I trusted my feet. Another obstacle I faced in the Kentucky marathon was a stomach ache. I started the race with it and felt it every step of the way. I could have opted not to start the race that day and I could have bowed out at any time. 26.2 miles is a long way to go with a stomach ache. But I kept going. I kept pushing forward, making the most of the day despite the pain.

In our writing lives, we do the same. A different set of obstacles emerge on each of our paths, and it is up to us to decide if we'll let the obstacle turn into a road block or if we'll find a way to navigate through it. I recommend the latter. Every time we overcome an obstacle, we fill ourselves with courage. We learn. We move forward, and our craft is better for it.

## INVEST IN THE RIGHT EQUIPMENT

The *right* equipment varies for each of us, based on our specific goals. A marathon runner who plans to run not one marathon, but twelve, understands the importance of trustworthy equipment. The runner who plans to run one may not view the equipment as such an important investment.

For most of us, running a marathon requires a sturdy pair of running shoes (likely several pairs while training, and possibly a separate pair of racing flats). Not only do we want the shoes to be sturdy, we want just enough cushion, too. Some of us need orthotic inserts. We need socks that don't bunch (if they do, we'll be plagued with blisters). We may need a trusted podiatrist. Elite athletes may hire agents. Marathon runners need comfortable running clothes for varying climates. We need a timer/watch/GPS. We need to know when to take in calories on a run and what specific calories are most beneficial (and to carry the calories we need packs). We need water bottles we can easily hold in our hands for a dozen or more miles. The point is, all marathon runners, regardless of competitive level and goals, need trustworthy equipment. Training for and running a marathon with a comfortable, reliable way to carry your water bottle and other calories can make a big difference in your performance.

In our writing careers, we need to take the same approach. If you are actively jump starting your writing life to build a long-term career, professionalism matters. And investing in the right equipment can help you in the professionalism arena. There are no right or wrong answers here. Find what works for you. Do you prefer writing with Scrivener? Do you use Vellum for interior formatting? If you're an indie author producing print books, do you use a print-on-demand supplier such as Ingram? Are you investing in the right editors? Traditional and indie authors need editors. Not only should you be careful to hire the proper type of editors for your work, hire the editors you work best with. Finding the best editor for your book is a bit like dating. It takes time to meet the right one and develop a relationship built on trust. Take time and careful consideration to invest in the right equipment and in well-trained professionals. Remember, when creating a writing life, you are the C.E.O. You decide who to hire. You decide which programs work best for your company. All too often I hear from aspiring writers who want to short-cut the process, convinced they can do everything themselves. You are the writer. They are the editors. They are the book cover designers, the interior formatters, the professionally trained audiobook narrators. Be a professional. Invest in the right equipment for your writing life. And collaborate with professionals.

## BE FLEXIBLE

Short- and long-term goals are a must. But so is flexibility. How can goals and flexibility co-exist? While training for a marathon, runners create a training plan; one week builds on the next. You don't start training for a marathon with a 30-mile run. You might start with running 30 miles in a week (and then you build your mileage up each week from that point on). There is a set plan that leads up to the marathon race day, in order to adequately prepare the body and mind for what it is about to endure. However, during each week of training, runners assess how their body is feeling (e.g., aches, pains, injuries) and adjust their training schedule as needed. While one marathon runner might need to run 100-miles each week, another may only require 60-mile weeks. Training differs for every runner. And the type of runs performed during each training week also vary (one runner may do several fast-paced work-outs, while the other may focus on long, slow and steady runs).

Not only is flexibility essential while training for a marathon, it is also part of the survival requirements while racing the marathon. If a marathon runner has a stomach cramp and needs to stop and stretch, they do what they need to do, and then hop back in the race.

In our writing lives, we need to exercise flexibility in the same way a marathon runner does. We set our writing plan (i.e., daily and weekly goals, long term goals) and we write. We get to work. But when we are faced with burn-out or if we fall ill, we take a minute to "stretch" before hopping back in the race. And as soon as we're able to so, we're back in the mix of things, plugging away, working toward our goals. If we refuse to be flexible and push through the flu, setting ourselves at the computer to write, we likely won't produce quality work during that time, and we are potentially setting ourselves up for failure or a bout of burnout.

## LEARN FROM FAILURES

Failures are really just experiences. They are opportunities to learn and grow. A supporter of my work once told me, "You always succeed at everything you do." I laughed, knowing this was absolutely not true. The truth was, she was only witness to those projects where I'd experienced success. She hadn't been party to the years of devastating set-backs, the heartaches, the disappointments, and the endless failures. She didn't know that I'd been writing most of my life. She didn't know I'd started submitting my novels to publishers at the age of 18, only to publish my first novel a full 16 years later.

Running a marathon has its own failures. I failed miserably when I flew to the Houston Marathon, in an attempt to run a qualifying time to The Olympic Marathon Trials. I failed with a big fat F. But I picked myself up, moved on and I learned. I learned plenty of lessons from that experience; one being, that nothing is ever a guarantee. We can work incredibly hard, train for years, and show up to the race and fail.

Where's the lesson in that? It reminded me to never take anything for granted. To be grateful for every bit of goodness that comes my way. And although on the outside, the race goes down as a failure, on the inside, I know the truth. On the inside, I learned plenty of lessons from that experience; lessons that carry me forward today.

As in the marathon, we need to learn from our failures in writing. There will be plenty for all of us. However, if we choose to focus on the good that each failure brings, instead of the negativity or embarrassment, we can emerge a stronger, more impactful writer. The first time I submitted a (paid) story to a newspaper editor, I mistakenly sent him an article about cats (something I'd written for our non-profit). When he pointed out my mistake I was mortified. To this day, I still check my attachments at least a dozen times before submitting my work to an editor.

## CELEBRATE EVERY MILE

In any marathon, celebrate every mile. You will learn something about your craft (and inevitably about yourself) each time you hit the next mile. Keep moving forward. You've got this! It's easy to breeze past the small successes without more than a brief nod of acknowledgment. The small successes fuel us with excitement, but they are all too easy to take for granted.

In our writing, we need to take time to celebrate the small things, too. Celebrate every day you make time for writing. It doesn't have to be in the form of a party (let's admit it, most writers are introverts who'd rather have a cup of joe with a friend, than join a houseful of guests at an extravagant party. Not true for you? Now I'm blushing, maybe it's just me!). Celebrate every time one of your articles is chosen for publication. Celebrate when you win awards. Celebrate when you publish a new book. Celebrate when your book hits the bestseller list. Celebrate when you outline your next book. Celebrate the gift of giving yourself time to rest between novels. Celebrate it all. After all, if we're developing a creative life we love, we should celebrate the fact we have the courage to go after our goals. Celebrating, not only the big milestones, but the small victories, will enhance and enrich our writing experience.

## ENJOY THE EXPERIENCE

Don't take yourself too seriously (I'm totally writing

this line as a reminder to myself!). In a marathon, we can speed through the training runs, and even through the race, neglecting to take in the scenery or to connect with those who cross our path. Or we can open our eyes and take a look around. We can glance up at the blue sky. We can take in the historic details on the houses in a neighborhood. We can stop to pet a cat who is sitting eagerly hoping for some attention. The choice is yours. How do you want to run *your* marathon (metaphorically speaking)?

In writing, we can apply the same principals. We can allow ourselves to fall victim to work-a-holic tendencies, or we can set realistic daily and weekly goals (e.g., word count goals) and provide ourselves enough time to stop and smell the roses along the way. As the C.E.O. of your writing life, you choose how to structure your business. I can tell you from experience, allowing yourself some time to stop and smell the roses is much more enjoyable.

## SURROUND YOURSELF WITH SUPPORTERS

Placing yourself in the company of those who support you and your goals, can go a long way. When I ran the Houston marathon, my family made a trip across the country to stand along the crowded streets and cheer. While the race didn't turn out as I'd hoped, I was grateful for their presence. In the aftermath of what I'd perceived to be a failure, it was encouraging to have loved ones by my side, reminding me of all of the good things I have in my life.

In writing, we benefit from the same type of support. Whether we experience a perceived failure or a well-earned accomplishment, having supportive friends, family, and colleagues by our side can alter our perspectives in a positive way and can push us to achieve new goals.

## MAKE NEW FRIENDS

Making new friends generally comes easy during our childhood. But when we're adults with busy schedules, families, responsibilities, and obligations, it can sometimes feel impossible to find time or energy to make new friends. As we jump start our writing career, it's important to remind ourselves to stay open to making new friends.

When traveling across the country to run road races, I made many unexpected new friendships. It is always interesting to learn someone's running/racing background, accolades, and experiences.

Furthermore, some of those friends have gone on to run professionally under sponsorships through Nike and others. It is exciting to follow their careers and to watch them succeed. Not only that, being open to making new friends helps us learn and grow.

In writing, we can make new friends in a number of ways. We can meet other writers at workshops, seminars, writing clubs, and when we join genre specific associations. We might beta-read another writers novel prior to publication. We may be solicited to read/review another authors novel on our book blog. We can co-author books. We make lasting connections with our professional editors, formatters, and book cover designers. Running marathons brings new friends, as does submersing ourselves in the world of writing. Befriending and/or collaborating with other writers helps us learn and grow our craft. In addition, it is a lot of fun to support one another along our unique writing journey's.

## CONGRATULATE OTHERS

When you get to the finish line, celebrate the victory. You've earned it! When you reach the finish line in a marathon you are filled with a mixture of elation and relief. You're both exhausted and grateful to have crossed the finish line. Your legs hurt. You're thirsty. Your eyes sting with tears and you're not sure if it's from the pain or the overwhelming satisfaction of a job well done. Regardless, you've done what you came to do. You accomplished your goal. Now you get to bask in that knowledge and congratulate others as they cross the finish line with the same look of exhilaration.

As a writer, it's equally enriching to pause after reaching a goal, celebrate your accomplishment and stop to look around and congratulate others. Take time to beta-read another authors book, or to read and post an honest review. You understand better than anyone, the hard work it takes to have your book published. Acknowledge the hard work put in by others, especially other authors in your niche. Doing so may lead to new friendships or collaborations. But you should take this action not for the reward it may yield, but to partake in the spirit of what it means to be a writer.

## REST, RECUPERATE, REPEAT

Rest. Recuperate. Repeat. Such is the life of a professional marathon runner. Such is the life of a professional writer. Just as marathon runners schedule much needed rest time after racing 26.2 miles, writers can benefit from scheduling down time after the completion of a novel. Not only will the down time recharge your writing juices, it will allow you to let go of the book you've just written. And it's crucial to let go of your book, before beginning to write the next one (that is, unless you're writing a series).

Take time to recuperate. Every marathon runner recuperates differently, and the same holds true for writers. I know marathon runners who take one week off from all exercise activities. Others take a full 4-6 weeks off after competing in a marathon, but they go to the pool to swim slow laps or they take a daily walk. Some runners prefer to get-away and take a week-long vacation following a race. Create a recuperation schedule that works for you.

Once you've given yourself adequate time to rest and recuperate, repeat the cycle. Start your next race. Start your next novel or writing project. If you're a marathon runner, you run. You run because you love it. If you're a writer, you write. And you write because it's who you are.

## AVOID BURN-OUT, STAY CONSISTENT WITH TRAINING

Are you ready to run a marathon? Maybe not. But hopefully you're ready to jump start your writing life. You'll experience much success if you keep reminding yourself, writing is a marathon, not a sprint.

In the marathon, runners avoid burn-out by practicing healthy daily habits, including self-care. In writing, we avoid burn-out by following the same rules. We stay consistent and dedicated to our daily writing (training) when we set a schedule, along with short- and long-term goals. Persistence cannot be underestimated. If we can stay consistent with our craft and avoid burn-out, we will be unstoppable.

# 4

## Which Route?

*"As a writer you try to listen to what others aren't
saying…and write about the silence."*

-N.R. Hart

Blaze your own trail. It's happened too many times
not to mention. Aspiring authors reach out to a friend
of a friend who is an author and they ask for *the
secret*. They want to be told how to be an overnight
bestselling author, and they want the answer to be
easy. The truth is, there is not a one size fits all
answer. Every writer carves their own path. It's part

of the beauty of living a creative life. We choose our own path. We choose what success means to us. While writers and creatives may inevitably intersect at various points along our journeys, no two journeys are ever identical.

Being the C.E.O. of our writing life, we need to make our own decisions. Certainly, we can learn from others. We can read blogs, articles and books. We can attend writing groups and seminars. But ultimately, we need to decide what works best for us. No one else can tell us the answer. We can support each other in our creative endeavors, but no one can tell you, do A, B, C, D…and so forth, and you'll be a multi-million-dollar bestselling author in nine months. It just doesn't work that way. Instead of searching for a secret formula, keep writing. Keep learning. Stay consistent and dedicated to your writing goals. If there ever was a secret to success, this is it. Just keep going.

Once you've established healthy daily habits and goals in your writing life, it's time to decide which route is for you. Will you write fiction or nonfiction? Will you utilize a traditional publisher? Will you be independently published, or will you take a hybrid approach? What is your niche and why? If you're a fiction writer, what is your genre? Will you hire an agent? An audio narrator? Which editors will you hire? Where will you find beta-readers for each book? Who will you hire as your cover designer? Your interior formatter? Will you hire a part-time or full-time assistant (e.g., to track numbers, assist with marketing efforts and social media, building an e-mail list, website maintenance)? Who will you hire as your web-designer? Whichever route you choose to publish your books (indie, traditional, or hybrid), you'll need a trusted editor and a marketing plan. Remember, no one cares about the sales of your book more than you.

Where will your books be available? Will your book be available to purchase by libraries? You can reach the widest audience by making your books available in the most places. In what countries will your book be available? Will you hire a translator for your books?

In what formats will your book be available to readers? eBook? Paperback? Hardback? Audiobook? The more available you make your book, the larger the pool of potential readers you will have. If you're indie published, will you only publish eBook's? If you're publishing print books, who will you use for your printer? Will you store hard copies of your books or use a print-on-demand service? How is the quality of the printer you are working with? If you're publishing via the traditional route, will you work with a big publishing imprint or a small press? What are the advantages and disadvantages of each, for your book?

Indie publishing has less stigma today than ever before. As an indie published author, you truly are the C.E.O. of your writing business. You can hire professionals (e.g., editors, formatters, cover designers, etc.) through independent contracting. You can conduct auditions with professional narrators around the world for your audiobooks. Successful indie publishing requires an entrepreneurial minded author; one who embraces both the writing and business life. Weigh the pros and cons of your options prior to taking the leap. There is no one right way to publish your books. Rather, as professional writers we must blaze our own path. We must make the decisions that work best for where we are in our writing careers. We must take into consideration our long-term writing goals. And we must not allow ourselves to fall into the fruitless search for an easy answer. If there was an easy button to becoming a bestselling author, everyone would do it. And after all, if we skipped the journey we would deny ourselves a creative existence. We would follow a set pattern and get a set result. What fun would that be? We are writers because we love to write. We need to write. We are writers because we have stories inside of us that we're longing to share with the world. We are writers because we have knowledge and experiences to share with readers. We are writers because we are creatives. And as creatives we long to create a life we love. Let's start creating. Let's start living the life we love, without excuses. Let's enjoy the journey and carve our own path along the way.

## 5

## Why Outline?

*"The most valuable of all talents is that of never using two words when one will do."*

*-Thomas Jefferson*

Why and how should we outline our book? Let's first start with why. An outline provides writers with a map. It allows us to gather our thoughts and organize them prior to delving into the writing of our full-length book. Not only does an outline allow us to gather our thoughts and place them into a logical, meaningful storyline, an outline also enables us to sketch out the scenes that inevitably bring the story itself to life.

An outline can be any number of things, and varies in its specific purpose from writer to writer. A few of the benefits I've found from outlining my own books are:

- Knowing my starting and ending points.

- A clearly defined setting.

- By sketching specific scenes, I can be sure the book moves at a good pace.

- Bringing the books characters to life prior to writing the book.

- Establishing the overarching theme or message of the story (making sure it holds true throughout).

- Allows the writer to play with the order in which the story is told.

- The outline provides a map to the writer. Once the outline is complete and you begin writing your book, you can set specific daily goals (e.g., write the first scene of chapter 2 today). For some writers, a scene goal can prove more beneficial than a word count goal.

- For nonfiction, creating an effective Table of Contents.

Now that we've explored why an outline is helpful to writers, lets jump into *how* to create an effective outline. But first, are you a pantser or a plotter? You're probably re-reading that question right now and asking yourself, *a what?* Hang with me. A plotter is a writer who utilizes an outline and plots their story prior to writing their book. A pantser, on the other hand, is a writer who does not outline or plan their book in any way. They "fly by the seat of their pants", so to speak. Do you know if you're a pantser or plotter? Have you tried writing a book each way?

Personally, I'm a hybrid of a pantser-plotter writer. Some people call us "plantsers".[1] For years I tried to write as a pantser. And for years I went unpublished in the book world. There were several factors involved here, but for me, pantsing wasn't cutting it. Now I outline my books, providing myself with a go-to map. But, for me, this doesn't mean I'm not inventing and creating along the way. Before I write a book, I know the title (it may change later, but usually it doesn't). For my fiction novels I know the intimate details of the setting (even if all of those details never make it to the actual book). I know my characters (their likes/dislikes, quirks, background…again, I know all of these details, even though many of the character details never make it to the actual book). I know my start and end points of the book. I have a mission statement for my book. I sketch out scenes and goals for each chapter, making sure the flow is agreeable to the pace and quality of the story. At times, I sketch into the outline, small details I want to be sure to mention in specific chapters (hints to drop) that connect and build the story. And then I get to work. As I write my book, with my outline somewhere close by, I am flexible and inevitably new details, scenes and outcomes pop up as I'm in the process of writing. This is how I take the "plantser" (aka hybrid) approach. It works for me, and so I've continued with it throughout the years. Of course, if in the future I make a tweak to my approach, I'm open to that if something begins to work better for me. The goal is to write a compelling story. The goal is to write a book that starts a conversation. The goal is to hold the readers interest. Whichever method allows you to do these things, use it.

For nonfiction, outlining a Table of Contents (and any subtitles which may be contained within each chapter) can be incredibly effective. I go a step further when outlining nonfiction and sketch out points to make, specific stories and examples to share, within each chapter).

Libbie Hawker,[2] author of *Take Off Your Pants! Outline Your Books for Faster, Better Writing* shared the importance of remembering that your characters have backstories. Unless your character is a newborn on page one of the book, your character has a backstory and it's important that the writer knows what it is. Furthermore, Hawker explained what most plotters get wrong when putting their outline together. "Plotters have it backward: the events in the plot must be created to force the protagonist to make a specific, really hard internal change. And that means you need to know, specifically, what the internal change will be before you begin creating a plot." Hawker emphasizes the need to demonstrate that the protagonist has a serious problem (internal, personal) they need to solve, and for her, the three benefits of outlining include: knowing the theme of the story, creating a character arc, and proper pacing.

Author Lisa Cron explains the following in her book, *Story Genius: How to Use Brain Science to Go*

*Beyond Outlining and Write a Riveting Novel*, "…often the very first scene in a novel includes a glimpse of what the ending will be." Take a look at some of your favorite fiction books. Does this statement hold true? Do you find, looking back at the first scene, that there are telling elements of the ending? Cron shares novelist John Irving's advice: "Whenever possible, tell the entire story of the novel in the first sentence." Difficult to do, but it does indeed make for an effective opening.

Are you convinced you're a plotter? Some writers argue that plotting takes away the creativity of writing. The fear of having to redo an entire outline, while you're in the middle of writing your novel (and you've hit a wall), is enough to keep some writers away from plotting entirely. While nearly all nonfiction writers outline in the form of a Table of Contents, not all fiction writers believe an outline is helpful. Pantsers argue that, without an outline, they are free to create the story as they go. However, the way I see it, I am creating the story in my head as I plot my outline. And I get to creatively add to that story as I write my book. Pantsers argue that if they decide they don't like a character while writing the book, they can decide to kill them off, whereas they see this as becoming more work if you've already written an outline. The New York Book Editors[3] agree with this argument, saying that writers should trust the process, and that less work upfront can mean more for your story during its writing (i.e., its creation). They mention trying to outline your book *after* writing your first draft. In essence, some writers believe your first draft *is* your pre-outline. They declare, "Don't plan. Write." And furthermore, "Your task is to create. The less you know before you start, the more you stand to uncover as you write." Others argue that outlining is simply another form of procrastination.

While outlining is not necessary for a story to be compelling, outlining in some form can enable writers to write faster and to be less prone to plot holes. Outlining can also allow writers to spot problems such as: character inconsistencies and pacing issues. In addition, when you know the end of the story, you can be sure to build up your tale with each new scene, and you can drop just enough (but not too many) clues along the way. There are countless ways to outline. What's important is to find which method works best for you.

For me, in addition to writing a loose and flexible outline I create a vision board of characters and settings for each of my fiction novels (hint: you can build this with a secret Pinterest board.). Other writers include character backgrounds (in the form of histories or in a Q&A format).

There are writers who swear by pantsing, others who strongly believe in plotting, and some who fall somewhere in between the two. It's important to remember there is no right or wrong way. If you're a pantser, awesome. If you're a plotter, terrific. If you're a plantser, super! The only mistake you can make is forcing yourself to be what you're not. If you try to be a plotter and you honestly work better as a pantser, most likely your story will fall flat before you can type *The End*. Stay true to who you are and what works best for you. Still don't know which camp you're in? Try writing a short story or a novel each way. Pay attention to which method (or mix of methods) work best for you and learn why it helps you, so that you can continue to benefit from the same method while writing your future books.

*"I'm writing a first draft and reminding myself that I'm simply shoveling sand into a box so that later I can build castles."*

-*Shannon Hale*

At minimum, as you begin writing your novel, it is

important to define your protagonist and the conflict (what problem is the protagonist trying to solve?). You don't have to create an outline, but knowing these two elements gives you a great start as you begin to write. Authors Jerry Jenkins and Dean Koontz[4] explain the basic story structure (this works whether you're a pantser or plotter) as:

1—"Plunge your main character into terrible trouble as soon as possible. *(That trouble will mean something different depending on your genre. For a thriller it might be life-threatening. For a romance it might mean choosing between two suitors.)*

2—Everything your character does to try to get out of the trouble makes it only worse.

3—Eventually things appear hopeless.

4—Finally, everything your character has learned through all that trouble gives him what he needs to personally conquer the opposition."

If you're new to outlining, consider starting small. Start by sitting down (or walking at your treadmill desk if you're lucky enough to have one!) and answering the following questions:[5]

- *Who is your main character?*

- *What central problem or conflict will they face in the novel?*

- *How will they solve this problem?*

- *What difficulties will they face when trying to achieve their goal?*

- *What are the main events within the novel?*

- *What type of novel will this be?*

- *What is the setting of the novel?*

Still unsure if you should give outlining a try? Thriller author Joanna Penn[6] explains the plotting method as: "It is basically the process of setting out the main events of your book and working out the plot from beginning to end. It can be a rough one-pager on how it all works, or a series of post-it notes put into an order for writing. It can also be a comprehensive meta-document that you refer to throughout your book and keeps you to the point. It is basically planning your novel before you write." Furthermore, Blake Snyder's bestselling book, Save the Cat! The Last Book on Screenwriting You'll Ever Need, while geared toward screenwriters, is filled with helpful information for all writers. The book doesn't specifically cover the in's and out's of outlining, but it does provide helpful hints and tips that can benefit writers of any method. In the end, whether you decide you're a pantser, plotter, or fall somewhere in between, writers can benefit from Snyder's teaching of the essential building blocks for good storytelling. Most importantly, writers benefit from knowing themselves. As I mentioned earlier in the chapter, I spent years pantsing my novels. And I spent those same years unpublished. Once I embraced the art of plotting (creating my own hybrid version of what some writers refer to as "plantsing"), my storytelling improved. I accredit this to a number of factors (not solely outlining, although it has undoubtedly been helpful). I began understanding the pace factor. I spotted plot holes faster. I built stronger, more efficiently told stories. In all, I found what worked for me. Once I began to embrace my writing style, everything started falling into place. Now it's your turn. What's your style?

## 6

## Getting Started in Fiction

*"No tears in the writer, no tears in the reader. No surprise in the writer, no surprise in the reader."*

-Robert Frost

### WHAT'S IT ABOUT?

"What's your book about?" I remember the first time I was asked this question of my fiction novel. I froze, a deer in the headlights. Generally smooth with my words, I couldn't get a sound to escape my lips. My brain raced. What *was* my story about? Of course, I knew what it was about. I'd spent a year writing it, working closely with editors, beta-readers and the like. I knew the story backward and forward, yet why couldn't I answer this one simple question? I was standing in front of an eager reader, a reader who was ready to buy my book...my first fiction book...and I couldn't seem to find the words to tell her what I'd spent all my time writing. Eventually a few words emerged from my throat. I felt my face grow flush with heat. I was mortified. At that moment, I was sure I didn't want anyone to read my book. I especially didn't want someone I knew to read my book! I'm not sure exactly how I answered the question that day, but what I am sure of is that I went home that night and promised myself that I would always have the answer from that point forward. Today, when someone asks, "What's your book about?" I'm prepared with a compelling twenty-second answer, hoping that if it's a book the questioner will enjoy, they'll feel intrigued enough to buy it.

I review books professionally and it is always clear when an author is confident in their book. What's also clear is if I'm compelled to read a book. The cover is important (we'll get into this more in Chapter 9). So too is the tag line. A tag line must hook the reader. A tag line (or thirty-second explanation) must draw us in. And in all honesty, thirty-seconds is a generous amount of time for someone to listen to your answer. The shorter and more compelling your answer to the question, "What is your book about?" the better.

I'll share an example. Here is commonly how I answer the question "What's your book about?" for my fiction novel, *All the Little Choices*. I reply with: "The book is a suspenseful drama. Tony and Abigail have the perfect marriage, until Abigail goes missing. The book is written in two voices, Tony (present day), desperate to save his wife, and Abigail (in the year leading up to her disappearance)." For my book, *Blink*, I often reply with: "One decision can change everything. At a crucial moment in her life, Casey Jane makes two very different decisions, both which have life-altering consequences that can't be stopped. Have you experienced a moment in your life where you've wondered, *what if*?" Here's another example. Author Randi M. Sherman explains her novel, *The Lobby*: "Meet and laugh with dozens of new friends in the elegant surroundings of The Shipley Hotel's lively lobby...The Lobby invites the reader to eavesdrop on the comings, goings and constant activity in the lobby of an upscale hotel in San Francisco." How will you explain your book to those who ask, "What's it about?" Can you keep it under thirty-seconds? Try it out on a few friends, co-workers, and neighbors and see if they're intrigued with your reply. Potential readers will be happy to share their feedback.

## WHAT'S THE FORMULA?

"A few years ago, in a writing class I ran, a student asked me to give her my 'formula' for writing publishable novels, and when I told her there was no such thing, she was most put out, saying, 'I suppose it's got to stay a secret for you published authors, doesn't it?' Nothing I could say could convince her otherwise" wrote Sophie Mason for *Writer UnBoxed*.[1] My inbox is flooded with similar inquires each week boasting subject lines such as: "Favor, please" and "Please Help ASAP!" Regardless of the clever (or not so clever) subject lines, most are searching for an answer to the same question: *how do I become a full-time author?* Or *I want to work from home. Who do I need to contact to become an author?* The bottom line is, there is no easy one-size fits all answer, at least not one that most people want to hear. If you truly want the easy answer, here it is: work your ass off day after day, and write because you love to write. As much as everyone wants a simple, easy-to-do answer, the one I just provided is not what most people want to hear.

(And as a side note to 'who do I need to contact?' There is not one person to contact when you want to write for a living. You'll need to contact plenty of people, yes. Editors. Proofreaders. Cover designers. Formatters. Marketing professionals. Agents. Publishers. Readers. But no one can tell you exactly who those people will be for you.) Being a writer takes you on a journey of discovery; discovery of your own unique path to creating a writing life for yourself.

While there is not one specific contact to "set you up" as a professional author, there are a few things you can do to strengthen and enhance your fiction writing right now:

- Join a local writing group
- Become a member of genre specific association (e.g., Romance Writers Guild, Dog Writers Association)
- Writing exercises
- Submit short stories to literary magazines
- Write for a local news source
- Blog
- Provide copywriting for websites

- Co-write a book with another author

- Remember to use any writing opportunity or activity as a chance to strengthen your storytelling skills.

*"Character is not created in isolation or repose; it's forged through interaction with others and the world."*

*-David Corbett*

## THE HERO'S JOURNEY

While there is no one way to tell a story, NPR's Ted Talk Radio Hour[2] hosted an intriguing podcast titled, "The Hero's Journey". The podcast posed the question, "Why are we drawn to stories about heroes? And what do they tell us about ourselves?" Host Guy Raz discusses the theory of The Hero's Journey throughout the episode, sharing that Joseph Campbell stated, "There is a blueprint encoded in storytelling." Furthermore, Campbell stated that there is a three-act rule, meaning that every heroes story follows the same three acts (in this order): 1- Initiation (the hero lives a normal, boring life. He/she has a call to action which seems to alter the hero's destiny). 2- Departure (the hero leaves home and goes on a quest). And stage 3- Return (the hero returns home having learned something). Raz shares that *Star Wars* follows The Hero's Journey. Why does the given pattern work time and again? Raz explains: "The pattern of events resonates in some way with the human experience. Because at some point in our lives we all face the challenge of finding out who we are, and what we really want." The story pattern works because we can relate. "In essence, the Hero's Journey says: in saving ourselves, we can save the world." And this is a message we gravitate toward.

> *"If you can create a key moment in the novel where something special or intense or important passes between the protagonist and this secondary character, it will do wonders for your story. So many moving, poignant scenes in movies are ones where the two friends have a moment like this. It feels sometimes like a beat or pause in the story, being more reflective and slower paced. But it adds heart, and that's what this is all about."*

> *-C.S. Lakin*

## EMOTIONAL CONNECTION

Are you – the writer – emotionally connected to your work (to your storytelling/writing)? If you are not emotionally connected to your work, your readers certainly won't be. No tears in the writer, no tears in the reader. Passion for writing- or whatever your calling – cannot be taught. Passion is the foundation on which you will build your writing life. Without it, storytelling will be difficult. Beyond your own passion for storytelling, you must be compelled to write the story. If you're struggling with your fiction writing, ask yourself: am I writing this book because I'm emotionally connected to the story? Or, am I writing this book because I think it's a "sellable" story? If your answer is the later, there's your problem. Toni Morrison said it perfectly, "If there's a book that you want to read, but it hasn't been written yet, then you must write it." Write the book you want to read.

Beyond this, realize that emotion is evoked in the reader through the protagonist (main character) of the story. Emotion is derived from how the protagonist is making sense of what's happening in their world. This holds true regardless of from what P.O.V. (point of view) the story is told (e.g., first person, third person). Lisa Cron, author of *Story Genius: How to Use Brain Science to Go Beyond*

*Outlining and Write a Riveting Novel* explained, "Anything that doesn't impact the protagonists internal struggle…will stop the story cold." Therefore, we can understand that to evoke true emotion from our readers (which is part of what we, as readers, are all seeking) we must:

- Establish a likeable, trustworthy protagonist *(by the way, protagonists with flaws are always more likeable and relatable).*

- Establish the protagonists internal struggle *(what is it, why is it, what do they risk losing by trying to overcome it, what would they have to do, that they cannot at this point, to overcome the internal struggle).*

- Be emotionally connected to the story *(as the writer).*

Allowing the reader to experience your character's human connections (and closeness) is a non-negotiable in fiction storytelling. That is why we open the book. We want to connect. We want to experience life in someone else's shoes, without the risk. We want to learn lessons that we can apply to our own lives. Cron writes "…what we keep most hidden about ourselves is exactly what we're dying to know about others…because it's such a relief to find out we're not the only one who feels that way. Even more liberating is the discovery that what we've always seen as negative in our own life might actually be a positive."

Another important point to remember, as Kristin Lamb explained, "Great fiction is always fueled by bad decisions and human weaknesses." It is indeed. No one wants to read a book about a perfect protagonist void of any and all flaws, who sails through life with no issues whatsoever. Boring. We want to read about experiences. We want to be with the protagonists as she takes action to overcome an internal struggle. We want to experience how her poor decisions and weaknesses get in the way of her goals. We want to like her and root for her. We want to be invested in the story as a reader. We want you, as the writer, to keep us turning the pages. We want you, the writer, to keep us guessing. To keep us intrigued until the very end.

When working to establish an emotional connection, never judge your characters. *Never.* If you judge your characters, it will show in your writing. Instead of judging them for their weaknesses or poor decisions, try empathizing with them. When writing, remember how you think and feel as a reader (if you're a writer, you should be reading a lot!). Readers like to be shown, not told. We don't want to be told that character A is terrible and character B is wonderful. We want to witness how they live their lives and make that decision for ourselves. As readers, we know that things are not often as they seem at first glance. Just as in reality, individuals have their own reasons for acting and behaving the way they do in various situations. Let us see these things in your characters. Grant us this privilege and we will grant you our raving reviews and loyalty as readers of your future books.

Adding a dose of humor is always a welcomed reprieve. You don't have to be writing a romantic comedy or even a humorous piece to add a spot of humor within your story. Matthew Quick's *Silver Linings Playbook* utilizes humor effectively, for example.

We write a book to start a conversation. Allowing your readers to emotionally connect with your characters and story will do just that. It will hook and pull us in. When we finish the book, it will leave us considering and thinking about our own lives. If we felt the emotional connection, a good book will inspire us to post on social media and tell our friends to grab a copy of the book, too.

*"People are hungry for stories. It's part of our very being. Storytelling is a form of history, of immortality too. It goes from one generation to another."*

-*Studs Terkel*

## BETWEEN THE WORDS

Words matter, they really do. After all, as writers, words are our primary tool. They're what we use to create our little worlds. They are our superpower. But in all honesty, big fancy words don't make you a memorable writer, your storytelling ability does. It's what's between the words that makes us feel (*remember everything we talked about in the Emotional Connection section?*). Both aspects are crucial to a well-written story. You must know how to work well with words, but you must also understand how to effectively tell a story. If you're lacking one of the two skills, your writing will suffer.

Does your story contain scenes showing (not

simply *telling* us about) human connection? This is an example of what occurs between the words on the page. Is your protagonists internal struggle intriguing and compelling? These are things that occur between the words. I spent many years of my life as an elite distance runner. As a runner, I'd read that you know you're enjoying the run when you forget you're running. The same truth applies to reading. Your reader is thoroughly enjoying the story once they forget they're reading words on a page. Once the reader is visualizing the characters, you're doing your job as a storyteller.

Furthermore, you can achieve the goal of both utilizing words and a mesmerizing storytelling ability by tossing the reader directly into human conflict from the first sentence of the story. *The Bestseller Code: Anatomy of the Blockbuster Novel* (by Jodie Archer and Matthew Jockers) shares: "...knowing how to write a winning novel is throwing us straight into human conflict." Archer and Jockers site the opening line of John Grisham's, *The Rainmaker*:

*"My decision to become a lawyer was irrevocably sealed when I realized my father hated the legal profession."*

The opening line of Grisham's novel lets us know, immediately, that the protagonist isn't crazy about his career as a lawyer and that he is submissive to his father. After one sentence we're intrigued. We're hooked. We find ourselves wondering, quite simply, *why? How?* And *who is the protagonist? What is his story?* Utilizing the power of what lies between the words, from the first sentence of your novel, will captivate readers.

*"For every important moment, your character needs to react. First viscerally, then emotionally, then physically and finally, intellectually. Often a writer will show a character reacting with deep thought about a situation, when their first natural reactions are missing."*

*-C.S. Lakin*

## INCREASE YOUR STORY'S TENSION

Your story's tension matters. What is tension? It's what keeps readers turning the pages. Tension is the anticipation of what will happen next. It's what pulls us into the story. It's a problem we want to see solved. It's an answer we need to know. It's a love triangle and we need to know who is going to end up with who. It's the protagonists internal struggle and we're rooting for him to overcome it. Tension is necessary to any good story. The human brain does not like to leave problems unsolved, and in a book, tension is the demonstration of exactly that. That's why cliffhangers work so well. If we care about the characters and we enjoy the story, a good cliffhanger will leave us longing for more. But tension doesn't only apply to books written in a series. Standalone books need tension, too. Every story needs tension. Otherwise, what are we trying to figure out? We are reading to go on an adventure without leaving the comfort of our pajamas. We are reading to experience life through someone else, while not having to personally suffer the consequences of their decisions (or indecisions). As much as we think we dislike tension, when it comes to reading, we love it. We long for it. We want to be hooked, and that requires tension.

Think about a few of your favorite books. What is the tension in the story? How does the author build up tension as the story progresses? Does he/she use cliffhangers at the end of chapters, to keep you awake a little longer at night…leaving you (the reader) with the *"just one more chapter"* syndrome?

*InkandQuills.com* shares five effective ways to increase your stories tension:

- "Don't let your characters have what they want."

- "Ask how you can make your characters' situation worse."

- "Build conflict into your setting/story world."

- "Create conflict between your characters."

- "Increase the consequences of failure for the hero."

Yes, it sounds cruel to not let your characters have what they want. I agree. But it's what works to create a good story. If we sat down to read a book and realized from the first page that the protagonist had everything they wanted, that there was no internal conflict – no tension – why would we want to keep reading? What more would we want to know? The answer is we wouldn't. We would likely put the book down and move on to the next one. James Joyce said it best, "Life is too short to read bad books." Don't let your book fall into this category (of course, you can write the most brilliant, clever book and they will always be some who won't enjoy it. Tell the world the sky is blue and some will argue that it's pink. We all have had different life experiences and when we read a book, we have thoughts and opinions based not only on the story itself, but on the lessons from our own personal experiences, too).

The basic premise of increasing tension in your story is to create problems for your characters. Place obstacles in their way. Create internal struggles. Show us what your character wants and why they can't have it (or what they need to overcome or face to try and get it).

Another way to increase your stories tension is through compelling combinations. What is a compelling combo? It's a pair of oddly mixed topics. Remember, we are writing a story to start a conversation. What better way to start a conversation than to allow your story to explore both faith and sex, or children and guns.[3] Authors Jodie Archer and Matthew Jockers share that emotional and ethical topics are "highly favored book topics". In addition, if the topics touch on something many of us fear, generally, the story becomes more appealing to us as readers. There are many books centered around this type of fear, focusing on accidents. Hospitals. Surgeries. Lawsuits. Jodi Picoult's books are excellent examples of this. *Small Great Things* focuses on race. *Nineteen Minutes* is written about a school shooting. *Change of Heart*, about the death penalty. How will you create tension for your characters? What will you do to increase the tension as the story moves forward? What consequences will your character's face?

> *"An author should know their character intimately, they should know their history, how they would react in a situation, they should know their look and mannerisms down to the smallest facial tick. Yet all of this need not be revealed to the reader."*
>
> *– Aaron Miles*

## DEFINING VOICE

Know your characters. Every story needs a protagonist because they are who the reader will see everything through. The protagonist is the one who leads us through the story (the adventure). Remember, reading is an experience. And to have this experience, we need a guide. That guide is the protagonist. It doesn't matter how you write the story (e.g., first person, third person), the guide (to the readers' journey of the story itself) will always be the protagonist.

Another important aspect to remember when writing fiction is to stay true to your characters' voice. This means not only in dialogue, but also in the characters' internal dialogue, thoughts, as well as in their actions and inactions. Consistency with character voice is imperative to good storytelling (just as is true with the narrator's voice).

How is a character's voice defined? It's defined through personality. Through who they are. Portraying a realistic character voice and tone are important to the story. Remember, it's the protagonist who we see the story through. We're rooting for them. We see why certain things upset them and others elate them. If you don't give them a realistic voice, one that is true to their personality, how can we, the reader, trust them to properly navigate us through the story? Once you've had a chance to develop your characters- whether through written character narratives, histories, and backstories, through outlining, or through simply seeing them in your mind- voice will develop soon after.

*"Give your characters a physical action to do based upon their emotions. This will look different for every character, just like it looks different for every human."*

-*Casey Herringshaw*

## DIALOGUE

Don't forget to let your characters speak. Dialogue is crucial. It's easy to fall into the trap of telling us what the reader is thinking or doing, or what they've done in the past. However, the present moment matters. And dialogue matters, too. We want to hear what the characters have to say. This is how we get to know them. Dialogue can be compelling, especially when we know what one character is saying to another, is not what they're *actually* thinking or feeling (ah-ha! This little trick can also add tension to the story!). In my novel, *All the Little Choices*, early in the story, readers notice that Abigail (the protagonist) is overwhelmed with the many changes in her life. She picks an ongoing fight with her husband, Tony, over his old La-Z-Boy chair. She wants to toss it and replace the old chair with something new; something better. The careful dialogue she utilizes to explain to her husband why it's time to replace the chair, isn't really about the chair at all. It's part of what makes dialogue such a compelling faucet of storytelling. We love hearing people's words and deciphering if they match their thoughts and feelings. That is precisely what tells the *real* story. Without character dialogue, we miss out on this type of decoding that we enjoy so much.

Dialogue is also a helpful factor when it comes to the pacing of our story. Dialogue keeps the story moving forward (or at least, it should). Dialogue keeps the reader engaged. Think about it. Would you rather read an entire novel on someone's thoughts, or would you rather read a story which includes character's (many times, multiple characters) thoughts, dialogue, actions, etc.? When I look back at the novels I mailed (I realize that by saying "mailed" I'm aging myself!) to publishers and agents when I was nineteen years old, I always notice the missing dialogue. There was dialogue in the books, of course, but there wasn't much of it. I focused too much on *telling* (oops! I should have been *showing*) the reader the characters' thoughts. *Telling.* And I failed to include much dialogue. And you guessed it, the pace of my stories at that time was slow. No wonder those early stories went unpublished.

When it comes to the pace of a story, keep in mind, generally, dialogue leaves more whitespace on the page. Why am I telling you this? Because, when there is more white space on a page, we generally read the page faster. And generally, there is more whitespace on a page toward the end of thrillers. The pace of the story picks up. We can't turn the pages fast enough (we're dying to know what's going to happen next: tension!). "Turn to a random page and take note of what you see. Is the text on the page dense with long expository paragraphs and little space between lines? Or, is the text more broken up, including shorter paragraphs, dialogue (fiction), subtitles (nonfiction), and plenty of space between lines? White space is just what it sounds like: the white space left on the page around the words," explains Susan Windsor Freeman.[4] She adds, "White space is refreshing, and it helps prevent readers from losing their place when they look away from text momentarily... If there is too much white space, then the piece looks unprofessional. If there is too little white space, then the reader has a hard time keeping their place. In fiction, different styles and genres of writing allow for less white space. What's right for one piece of writing may not be right for another. In some cases, it likely comes down to intuition on the author's part."

Dialogue between characters helps us navigate the story world. It picks up the pace in a story. It (if we utilize it correctly) keeps readers intrigued. Readers want to hear what the characters have to say as much as we want to see what actions they're going to take to solve whatever predicament we've placed them in this time. The bottom line is, do not underestimate the importance of dialogue in your story.

*"Think of your character as a jewel that has about a thousand different facets. If you keep turning them over and exploring new sides, you'll keep discovering new information about their personality and motivations. And there's always another way to turn things. There's always another side to explore."*

*-Lauren Sapala*

## CONFLICT

Good novels start in the middle of conflict. Show your readers, from the start, that your protagonist has an internal struggle that is going to last the length of the story. You might be thinking to yourself right now, wait, didn't we already discuss this? Isn't conflict the same as tension? Author K.M. Weiland blogged about this very topic, writing that tension and conflict are "…kissing cousins that fulfill similar functions within the story."[5] Weiland goes on to explain:

"*Conflict* indicates outright confrontation. Two people arguing. Two armies fighting. Or even something slightly less aggressive, such as someone who desperately needs money losing their winning lotto ticket. *Tension*, on the other hand, is what I like to think of as the *threat* of conflict. You'll have tension in a scene in which your characters are hunkered down in a bunker waiting for the next artillery bombardment. You won't have any actual conflict in this scene, since nothing is actually happening to the characters. But you do have plenty of tension because characters and readers alike know something is *about* to happen."

Take a look at the novel you're currently working on (or one you've just completed). What conflicts do you include in your novel? How do they differ from the tension? Does your novel contain both? Do you have conflict *or* tension in every scene of your story? Do the two balance each other out? Keep in mind, you don't want to have conflict in every scene, otherwise your story will become monotonous. That's where tension comes in. Tension builds the pressure. It puts stress on your protagonist. It makes us wonder. Tension is a way of dialing down your story without boring the reader.

*"Good characters are why most people read, I think. However, in order to create a character people want to be BFF with, the characterization is secondary. In fiction, plot reveals character."*

*-Joe Bunting*

## KEEP THE READER HUNGRY

What is it that the reader wants to know? Why should we keep reading your book after the first sentence? The first page? The first chapter? The seventh chapter? The second to last chapter? Keep the reader hungry for more. Not just once, but throughout the story. Answer the above questions for every scene you write. In every scene, ask yourself, why will the reader care about this?

Authors Archer and Jockers explain as writers, we

must do the following within the first ten pages of a good novel:

- "Increase the heartbeat of the reader."

- The reader must "feel anxiety in the gut."

- "Feel a stirring arousal/back of the neck prickle."

- "Smile."

They add, "you must hook your reader by making them feel!" Keeping a reader hungry goes beyond the first ten pages of your novel. However, you can utilize aspects of the list above throughout the story. We always want to keep the reader wanting to know what happens next (that's keeping them hungry). We achieve this through a creative combination of tools (e.g., dialogue, the protagonists internal struggle).

Think, for a moment, about some of your favorite books. What was it you wanted to know? What kept you reading? What kept you intrigued? Now think about your own writing. Are you utilizing the same tools as your favorite authors, to keep readers hungry?

*"Don't just use visual details, but also include kinesthetic details, or how the character moves. Graceful, limping, stutter-step, lumbers, waddles, stomps."*

-Darcy Pattison

## USING THE 5 SENSES

Engage your readers. Bring us into your story. How, you ask? Use the five senses. Take a moment to read your most recent story. It doesn't have to be a novel, it can be a short story. Take note, how many senses did you bring to the attention of the reader throughout your story? The more senses you can bring to life in your writing, the more engaging your writing can become. Why? Because incorporating the senses into our writing often evokes emotion. Let's explore how you can use each of the senses in your writing.

## SIGHT

Show, don't tell. As we've discussed earlier, don't tell us what you want us to see. *Show* us. (e.g., Don't tell us Claudia is sad. Show a scene with Claudia grabbing her heart and weeping). Allowing us to *see* what is happening (rather than being told), allows us to feel what the character is feeling in that moment.

## TASTE

"This might be awful, but my favorite way to describe what something tastes like is by use of a metaphor. My favorite comedian, Tim Hawkins, compares the flavor and taste of a Krispy Kreme donut to "eating a baby angel." How true is that though? My roommate describes her tomato soup like "just coming in from a blizzard, kicking your boots off, and sitting in front of the fire." The metaphors we use have the power to transport even our readers to places that evoke memories and emotion from their own life, allowing a deeper connection to be made," shares writer Kellie McGann.[6]

## TOUCH

Touch can be described through temperature and texture. For example, *"Claudia's toes bravely poked the edge of the frigid, choppy lake."* McGann explains, "When writing about touch, the physical is very important to describe, but even more important is the invisible. The different aspects that are "touched" but not with your hands."

## SOUND

Sounds can be external (e.g., the explosion of fireworks) or internal (e.g., a private thought). You can also incorporate sounds into your story with onomatopoeias (Dictonary.com defines onomatopoeia as: "The formation of a word, as *cuckoo*, *meow*, *honk*, or *boom*, by imitation of a sound made by or associated with its referent."). Sounds can bring a sense to life, allowing the reader to experience the noise of the busy traffic on the street.

## SMELL

Smells can be used to describe things that smell (e.g., *"The room filled with the aroma of fresh lavender"*). However, smell can also be used to explain situations (e.g., *"I watch from the safety of the porch as the rain pours down in sheets, leaving the air that lingers between us smelling like summer as it wisps against my fragile skin"*).

As you describe the various senses throughout your story, keep in mind that they work best when the reader realizes why the character is describing that particular sense and what it means (i.e. under the topic of touch, when the example given is: *"Claudia's toes bravely poked the edge of the frigid, choppy lake,"* the reader realizes that the usage of frigid and choppy are not warm and happy terms. Rather, they indicate trouble and an internal struggle of some type. Possibly depression.). As readers, we are constantly working to gather clues. We take clues from the descriptions of the senses, too.

> *"You must learn to be three people at once: writer, character, and reader."*
>
> -Nancy Kress

## KNOW YOUR AUDIENCE

Think of yourself as a reader first. This is how you begin getting to know your audience. Remember, as a reader, you come to expect certain things from certain authors. A light read. A hold-your-breath suspense. A big twist at the end. Even if your favorite author writes under one name for a variety of genres, still, you know their sound and tone. You know their voice. In fact, in many ways you might feel that you know *them*. What do (or will) your readers expect from you? What does your tone of (writing) voice say about you as an author?

What will you do to build the trust of your audience? Did you know, on average, most readers won't remember the title of a book, but they will remember an author's name? They will remember an author's name, that is, after having read and thoroughly enjoyed at least three of their books (side note: many authors stop writing at or before they publish three books). One thing you can do to earn the trust of your readers is to keep writing. The more books you have available (especially when they're written on one specific topic) to readers, the more likely you are to be discovered. And the more likely you are, as an author, to have a new reader take a chance on one of your books. In a sense, it's a free form of marketing. Only, we all know it takes a lot of time to write a novel, send it off to the editors, re-write the novel….and on and on and on until it's eventual publication. Nevertheless, you will build the trust of your growing audience if you continue to produce quality books on in a specific genre, that are written in your unique tone and voice. We live in a culture of Netflix binging. We like to find a series (of books, shows, or even authors) that we enjoy and trust and then we binge. And that's exactly what we want our readers to do with our books; binge. Keep on writing!

As a survivor of sexual assault, I am incredibly sensitive to scenes that include rape, abuse and extreme violence (for years, I've wished there were disclaimers on books that contained these elements!). I am careful to read through reviews prior to purchasing a book, hopeful, that if the book contains such a scene, that a thoughtful reviewer will provide a disclaimer in their write-up. As much as I do this, every month I stumble across several books that surprise me in this unpleasant way. I'll be reading along, really enjoy the story and then boom. There's one of *those scenes*. It's difficult for me to digest. Sometimes the scenes are so descriptive I close the book at that point, never to open it again (even if it was a great story). This type of scene ruins it for me, and I'm an avid reader of books in a wide variety of genres and topics. I'll jump down from my soap box now. My point is, be kind to your audience. Know who your readers are. If you write romances with happily-ever-after's, likely your readers spend time with your books because they enjoy an escape. They enjoy winding down at the end of a long work day. They enjoy when books evoke emotions such as happiness and light-heartedness. They don't open your book in search of dark and disturbing stories. They don't open your book to solve a mystery. *Why* your readers are attracted to your books matters. Why they're attracted to your books tells you what they're hoping to get from your future books. It also tells you, the writer, why the readers are putting their trust in you. It tells you exactly what it is they like about *your* writing.

Building a relationship with your readers (through words, of course), builds trust. And when readers trust you, they'll come back to you. They'll recommend you as an "author to read" to friends and co-workers. Remember, as writers, we work magic with words. We hold in our hands, the potential to shift someone's perspective. We have the possibility of expanding readers' capacity for empathy and compassion. We can provide readers with escape. With an adventure. Our words and books can instill a new-found confidence in others. The point is, words are magic and the way we string them together into a story can influence others, often in ways that we'll never be privy to. Realizing this, we need to use our words wisely and carefully. As writers, we have the amazing privilege of sharing our stories with the world. So, let's share our best stories with our readers. Let's write our hearts out and then keep writing some more, because we love doing it, and our readers love reading it.

*"Overly tragic back stories played up front are not the way. Characters' reactions and the way they deal with what's happening to them in the "here and now" tells us SO MUCH more than acres of flashbacks or expositional dialogue about their traumatic childhoods."*

*-Lucy V. Hay*

## FICTION AT ITS BEST

One of the best pieces of advice I've received when it comes to fiction writing is: "until we know what a character wants, we don't know what the story is about. And, until we know what the stakes are, we don't care" (author unknown). What does *your* character want? Have you let us know within the first page of the story? What are the stakes? Again, have you let us know?

Is your protagonist likeable? Are they flawed? Have you demonstrated those flaws? What are their strengths? Weaknesses? Human weaknesses, along with poor decisions (which create obstacles) are the fuel of good fiction novels. Remember, we love to learn when we read. And we especially love learning how others cope with flaws, weaknesses, and poor decisions (this makes the story relatable to reality). Including these elements in your story will serve to make your protagonist more appealing to readers.

Never show bias when writing a character. Readers don't want to be told what to think. We want to be shown the situation and make the assessment ourselves. We all arrive to a book with different life experiences and expectations. Don't assume that because you dislike a character's personality, that every reader will. Your job is to share their story, not to judge it. With every scene you write, ask yourself, why does this scene matter? Be sure every scene is contributing to the story, building upon the last scene and adding to the tension and/or conflict of the story.

Author Elizabeth Gilbert was a guest on Marie TV[7] and explained to viewers that as she's writing a book it's her *baby*. She coddles it, tends to it, fusses over it, etc. But once the book is published, she knows she must let it go. Gilbert said once her book is published, it is no longer *her baby*. At that point, it becomes a product. At that point, she explained, the book will take on whatever shape the reader thinks it does (and that shape may be different for every reader). It is out of the author's control. It's out of her hands. I mention this because I think it's important advice for every author to remember. We pour our hearts and souls into our writing. We are incredibly vulnerable. When I have a new book published, especially if it is one that shares some of my personal stories (such as my motivational book, *Be Awesome: How to Live Your Best Life*), I feel like I've been stripped naked on the street and I'm running around like a wild woman trying to find something to cover myself, while everyone is pointing and staring. It's incredibly uncomfortable. But nevertheless, we're writers, and that often means exposing our souls to the world. As difficult as it can be, our readers generally appreciate our candid honesty. They enjoy getting to know a little more about our private lives (about what makes us flawed and human). And then, even as we feel like naked people running around terrified in the streets, we must be able to answer the question (in thirty-seconds or less), "What is your book about?" If we can't do that, we probably won't sell many books. And correct me if I'm wrong, but I'm pretty sure we'd all like to sell more books. Another note on fiction writing, if you're struggling to define what genre you want to write (or even if you're just curious about facts and figures in the writing world), check out *AuthorEarnings.com*. The site is operated by authors, for authors and aims to share information to help authors make informed decisions.

Finally, never forget the important work you're doing. I consider myself incredibly fortunate to live a creative life. It's taken a long time to get here and it is an incredible amount of hard work, but I wouldn't trade this life for anything in the world. Whether you wish to write full-time or on the side of your day-job, you can jump start your writing life with the techniques presented in this chapter, and throughout the book. And when your first book (or your twenty-fifth!) is published, I'd love to hear about it. If you find the information in this section helpful, I'd be so appreciative of an online review letting me know. I am delighted when writers let me know my words, personal experiences and stories have helped them in some way on the journey to their writing goals. Always remember that your words and actions matter. Not just as a writer, but as a human being.

You have the power to impact so many others, even others you may never meet or know. Your words carry magic. Remember that.

> *"Writers aren't exactly people…they're a whole bunch of people trying to be one person."*
>
> *-F. Scott Fitzgerald*

## PEN NAMES

A pen name (nom de plume) is a pseudonym used by an author in replacement of their own name, on the cover and title page of their books. Why do authors use pen names? The reasons range, however here are a few reasons you may want to consider writing under a pen name for your fiction novels:

- If you write books in various genres (some authors prefer to use one name for each genre so that they can earn readers trust in a specific genre).

- To protect the author's identity (e.g., if you're a childcare provider writing adult thriller titles, you may wish to differentiate your identity).

- To overcome limitations of the author's real name (e.g., if you don't like your name or feel it's too long, if you want to disguise your gender, etc.).

Keep in mind, creating a pen name (or names!) creates a lot of extra work. Two of every social media page. Two websites. Two e-mail newsletters. Two author bios. Author Belinda Pollard[8] weighs in on the topic, adding, **"Once upon a time, publishers tended not to allow their authors to write in conflicting genres and styles.** They wanted them to maintain a consistent *author brand*. If you have an agent, they may insist on this. Such a policy means that any other types of writing have to appear under a different name, so they don't confuse the brand. **But some are now finding that the policy is relaxing a little**, and authors are being given more freedom to explore all the different types of things they long to write." Furthermore, Pollard explains: "Audiences seem to be increasingly flexible in coping with such mischief. Let's face it, sometimes the person who loved your book on building a better rabbit hutch also happens to like cozy mysteries, and will buy your tale of murder because they enjoy your authorial voice!"

On a personal note, I began my author career with a line of nonfiction books on animal welfare. As the co-founder and Executive Director of Advocates 4 Animals, Inc. I'd established myself as an expert in the field. When my first two fiction books were published, they were under a pen name. The thought was, my animal welfare readers weren't going to be interested in my fiction (contemporary romance) novels. However, we quickly learned that many of my readers *wanted* to read my fiction books (and any other books I published, in any genre). They wanted to know what *I* was writing next. I was flooded with questions of "*why* are you using a pen name? Do you know someone by *that* name? Are *they* the co-author of the book? Are *you* their ghost writer? How can I find *your other* books?" The pen name for my fiction novels died in a year's time. I now write all of my books under my given name, Stacey Ritz. While I admittedly write on multiple topics (*Motivation/ Inspiration, Writing, Animal Welfare, and Fiction – love stories*), it works best for me to keep it simple and to not use a pen name. My readers are happy and

I'm happy. But it took some trial and error first to discover this.

As with everything in writing, the choice to use a pen name is different for every writer. Are you considering a pen name? If so, take time to consider the pros and cons of a pen name for your writing life. There are plenty of authors who use pen names and are wildly successful. J.K. Rowling also writes under the name Robert Galbraith. Nora Roberts also writes as J.D. Robb. Agatha Christie also wrote as Mary Westmacott. Dean Koontz writes under ten different names, including: Aaron Wolfe, Brian Coffey, David Axton, Deanna Dwyer, John Hill, K.R. Dwyer, Leigh Nichols, Anthony North, Owen West, and Richard Paige.[9]

*"I've been thinking about that word compassion and how it's achieved in fiction—about how, in fact, my favorite characters in literature are those mysteriously human enough to startle me into empathy. It's that word mystery that seems to be the point: The characters that most powerfully evoke my compassion are the ones who, paradoxically, most resist being known."*

*-Geoff Wyss*

# HOW TO AVOID COMMON MISTAKES IN YOUR FICTION WRITING:

- Proofread. Proofread. Proofread.

- Hire professional editors.

- Land as many eyes on your novel (beta-readers!) and as much feedback as you can prior to publication.

- Pay attention to the pace of your story.

- Hook the reader from the first sentence.

- *Always* show (don't tell).

- Utilize humor when possible.

- Know your characters backgrounds, as well as their goals, hopes, and dreams.

- Create a realistic (flawed) protagonist.

- Let us know (as soon as possible) what the protagonist wants (what is their internal struggle?). Until we know what a character wants, and what the stakes are, we won't care.

- Always increase your stories tension.

- Utilize dialogue!

- Be emotionally connected to your story.

- Be able to state what your story is about, in thirty-seconds or less (is it compelling?).

# Getting Started in Nonfiction

*"How vain is it to sit down to write when you have not stood up to live."*

-Henry David Thoreau

## WHAT'S YOUR TOPIC?

Are you an expert at knitting? Are you the founder and operator of a successful non-profit? The C.E.O. of a lucrative business? Are you a sought-out fitness professional? Where do you excel? What is your expertise? Do you have an author platform? An author platform is, as Jane Friedman explains, "...an ability to sell books because of who you are or who you can reach. Platform is a concept that first arose in connection with nonfiction authors."[1] If you're the head of a lucrative digital business, your book will appeal to many of your clients, and also to those who hope to have a career similar to yours one day. This means you have a platform. You have experience to share with your readers. And you have something to teach or impart on us.

Maybe you're a blogging expert who wants to help others become better at this task. Your author platform will include your blog followers, along with others who wish to improve their blogging techniques (e.g., business owners, entrepreneurs). You might be a motivational speaker wanting to share your lessons and stories with a wider audience. Are you knowledgeable and experienced in the topic you choose to write? If it's not already obvious, readers want to learn from doers. We want to hear firsthand stories and experiences from those who have lived them. We want to know what it's really like to escape a cult. We want to know how to start an organic farm from an actual organic farmer. Not from someone who has merely researched the topic. We can research the topic too, thanks to Google. What we want when we buy a nonfiction book is to hear from the experts. We want to learn from those who have been at the top of the game in their field of work. And it's not just facts we come to the book for. We come to the book to hear about you. We want to hear about your failures and struggles. We want to know what obstacles you faced on your own journey and what you did to overcome them. We want to know the good and the bad. We want to know the real deal. Nonfiction books cover a wide array of topics, but what they have in common is, they address a topic readers want to learn more about (from how to become a vegetarian to treadmill workouts for all levels of runners). Nonfiction books are an unspoken promise to readers that they will come away from the book with new knowledge.

Consider this. I could write an article on organic shampoo. I can research the benefits and include the facts in my article. But until I've tried the organic shampoo—or better yet, many versions of organic shampoo, I'll be missing a crucial element of the story. The reader wants to know the facts, yes. But in today's technologically advanced world, we can find facts nearly anywhere. We're reading the book to find the facts not only presented in an organized, easy to understand manner, but to also read about *your* experiences. We read fiction books to experience life through the protagonists' eyes. It's a risk-free way to take an adventure and learn a few lessons along the way. We read nonfiction books for similar reasons. We want to learn from the author in a risk-free manner. The author is the protagonist of a nonfiction book. We want to learn from your experiences, so that we might not make the same mistakes along our own journey.

So, what's your topic? And what is your author platform? What makes you qualified to write about this particular topic? Can you define an aspect about yourself that makes you uniquely qualified to write this book (i.e., what makes you different)? Before you begin writing your book, answer the above questions. They are crucial to your future success as a nonfiction writer. When you pitch a book to an agent they'll want to know your answers before they take the time to read your pitch. If you're plan is to be independently published, your readers will ask themselves the same questions before purchasing your book (e.g., Who is the author? Why should I listen to them on this topic?).

*"The sure sign of an amateur is he has a million plans, and they all start tomorrow."*

## MAKE A PLAN

Whether you work best as a plotter or pantser when it comes to outlining (or somewhere in between), when preparing a nonfiction book, it helps to prepare a T.O.C. (table of contents). Of course, if you benefit from a more in-depth outline, you can include additional details (e.g., subtitles within each chapter, stories and experiences to share broken down per section). It can also be helpful to prepare a mission statement for your book, as we discussed earlier. Remember, as authors we are entrepreneurs (regardless of which route we publish our books). And mission statements are crucial to the success of any business. A mission statement allows you to identify specific goals for your book. In addition, a mission statement can be one sentence or two-pages (whichever works best for you). The point is, to know your goal(s) for the book and keep them in mind as you're writing.

As the cofounder and Executive Director of an animal welfare non-profit organization, I co-wrote a book (with the cofounder of our organization) titled, *Covered in Pet Fur: How to Start an Animal Rescue, The Right Way*. At that point, we'd been operating our non-profit for more than a decade. "How can I start an animal rescue?" had become such a common question, coupled with the fact that we wanted to expand our reach of assisting others help homeless animals around the globe. Writing the book was a must for us. Prior to writing the book, however, we prepared our table of contents and discussed what stories, experiences, research, and statistics we wanted to share within each chapter.

When creating a plan for your nonfiction book, prior to writing, be sure to also plan what research and interviews you'll need to conduct. Keep track of your groundwork (Excel spreadsheets come in handy!), noting with whom you spoke, what they said, along with their contact information should you need to re-contact them to clarify any information. Careful notations are also important when building your bibliography.

Nonfiction books written in a well-organized, easy to digest manner, and those that include specifics on what we can do to work toward our goal (of whatever you're teaching us with your book), are appreciated by readers. Planning ahead will provide you with a roadmap as you begin writing your book.

*"I'm just going to write because I cannot help it."*

## WHY?

It's a simple question, but one that must be answered before sitting down to write your book. Why are you writing it? In the first section of this chapter (*What's Your Topic?*) we discussed qualifications for writing on your particular topic. But *why* are you writing the book? And furthermore, why *now*?

We wrote our book, *Covered in Pet Fur*, because we wanted to help others learn how to save animals. With more than three-million healthy, adoptable pets dying in animal shelters across the United States each year, we wanted to share our experience and knowledge with others who hope to volunteer for or to start an animal rescue. With our own local animal shelter having killed upwards of 80% of all pets who entered their doors (data: 2013), we wanted to let other animal lovers know the truth. More pets die of shelter euthanasia in this country, every year, than any illness or disease. We want to change this. We know that when we all work together, when we share what we know and encourage each other, we can do better. We have to do better for the animals. We want to help more animals than our own organization has outreach to help from our own tiny pocket of the world. And by sharing our experiences, knowledge and expertise with others (in our book), we are doing just that. The feedback we receive from readers around the globe is amazing. Our book is fulfilling the mission statement we wrote for it. It is helping to save more lives by motivating and inspiring others to help homeless, abused, and neglected animals. My first book, *Pawsitive Connection: Heartwarming Stories of Animals Finding People When We Need Them Most*, was written for much the same reason. The book shares stories of cat and dog rescues, rehabilitations, and adoptions from our organization. It shares stories of how animals miraculously overcame their past abuse and went on to help transform the lives of humans who found themselves in need. My goal was to share what animal rescue is and why it's needed.

Now it's your turn. Why are you writing your book? What are your qualifications? What are you bringing to the table to teach, share, and/or help others? Specifically, how are you helping them? What will your unique experiences provide for the reader?

When writing a nonfiction book, it can be helpful to start small. If you're hoping to write your first book, it may be beneficial to begin writing your advice and experiences in a blog format (and/or for local newspapers). This practice can help you build your author platform, while also building your writing skills. Writing in this manner will also teach you how to hook readers and keep them reading for the length of an article (an important skill to utilize in writing a book, too!).

> *"As a writer you should not judge, you should understand."*
>
> *-Ernest Hemingway*

## VULNERABILITY

Honesty and vulnerability matter. Readers buy your book to hear from you. We want you to share statistics and facts, but they also want to hear your stories and experiences. We want the unique aspect that is yours. Of course, we want to read about your accomplishments (likely that's why we've bought your book; because of who you are), but we really want to hear about your pitfalls and setbacks. We want to hear what you did to overcome them and what lessons you've learned along the way. We hope after reading about obstacles, we may minimize our own. It's similar to what we talked about in the chapter on fiction writing. We enjoy a protagonist who is flawed. Why? Because it makes him relatable. The same is true for nonfiction, only *you* are the protagonist of the story. Vulnerability is tough. It can make us feel embarrassed or less than, but it's also what makes us human. We can connect through vulnerability, because none of us are perfect. There is no such thing as perfect. We are all vulnerable to being less than perfect. When writing your book, always remember: vulnerability makes you relatable. And being relatable connects you to your reader.

I feel vulnerable every time I publish a new book. I want it to sell, but I also want to run and hide under the covers. It's hard to put ourselves out there. It's hard to know we'll be judged. It's terrifying to worry about reviews (e.g., will readers leave reviews? Will the reviews be positive?) We pour our heart and soul into our writing. We share a part of ourselves with our readers. And we have no idea who will pick up our book and read it. I think most authors will agree when I tell you that it's exciting, but also terrifying to know that your book is out, circulating in the world. When my book, *Be Awesome: How to Live Your Best Life* published I didn't sleep for a week. Three weeks after its release date, I wanted to unpublish it. I shared parts of myself in the book and I worried I'd shared too much. I felt exposed. I was waiting for reviews to be published, concerned that people would hate it. Prior to publication I'd received positive feedback from my beta-readers, editors, and proof-readers. Yet still, I tossed and turned at night. *What had I done?* I woke up one morning, my head filled with worry, only to receive a text from a friend, telling me what a great book it was. I hadn't known she'd purchased it and she went on to tell me she read it in two-nights and couldn't wait to read it again. She told me specifics of what she liked and how the book made her feel inspired and uplifted. I closed my eyes, took a deep breath and began writing my next book that day. Sometimes it takes a while to accept that we've put our art out into the world, for others to hold, to judge, to criticize, to enjoy. It can be overwhelming. But I can also tell you, it is worth it if you put forth your best effort. It is worth the effort, the worry, the strain, the fear. It is worth the vulnerability. Although at times, I promise you, it can be downright excruciating.

*"Happiness is a book you can't put down."*

## BE A READER FIRST

Why will readers be drawn to your book? What will

they learn? If you promise them something on the cover, be sure to deliver. Think about yourself as a reader. What nonfiction books do you read? Why do you read them? What do you like about them? Which books are your favorite? Why?

Several months ago, I read a book called *How Not to Die: Discover the Foods Scientifically Proven to Prevent and Reverse Disease* written by Michael Greger, M.D. Why did I read it? Below are a few reasons I chose to read this book:

- Clever title (caught my attention).

- Appealing cover (professional design).

- The author is a true expert (he is a physician and runs the website NutritionFacts.org).

- I'm interested in health and nutrition.

- I wanted to learn something new.

- I read a free sample prior to purchasing and enjoyed the tone and voice of the book.

- The information was presented in a clear and interesting manner.

- The book had good reviews.

A clever title, explaining what readers will get if they buy your book, cannot be overestimated in its importance. A professional, creative, appealing book cover is a must. The author is absolutely an expert in the field. I knew I would learn something from the author. He was a proven professional. I skimmed the reviews and they echoed what I'd hoped to hear. The author was indeed knowledgeable and presented the information clearly, making the content easy to grasp and implement. The voice and tone of a book matter, too. And the author's voice and tone were consistent throughout the book, which is always appreciated by readers. I generally look to see if the author has other books on the same topic. This one did not, however, it did not deter me as a reader because I trusted the author based on his noted experience. I also trusted him because of the professionalism in the way the book was presented (e.g., book bio, author bio, reviews, professional cover).

- What problem does your book aim to solve? What question are you answering? What do you want to help the reader with? Why?

- Can readers find you outside of your book

(on the same topic)? For example: other books on the same topic, as a speaker, a video series, website, blog, podcast, etc. Provide opportunities for your readers to find you elsewhere (this will also serve to enhance your author platform).

Keep in mind, as a reader, it feels good to be understood by the writer. How can *you* make your reader feel understood? (Remember: vulnerability makes you relatable) Always put yourself in the readers' shoes. Why would your book appeal to you? Would it catch your attention among the many other books written on the same topic? If so, why? If not, what can you do to change your answer to yes? It can be helpful to connect with your potential readers prior to writing the book. Ask those who are interested in your topic if they were to buy a nonfiction book, what information would they want to learn? Why? What would be helpful to them? What type of book would make them excited? You can learn a lot when you listen to your potential readers.

Something else you can do that has proven helpful to authors is to read the top ten bestselling books in your niche. Read them and find out why they are bestsellers. What information are they providing to readers? What do their covers look like? How is the information in the book organized and presented? Furthermore, spend time reading reviews written on the top ten bestsellers. Read the five-star reviews and the one-star reviews. Both will tell you what readers liked and disliked about the books, helping you in the creation of your own book (i.e., can you better address a topic that readers of the bestsellers felt wasn't covered well enough?).

*"Writing is an exploration. You start from nothing and learn as you go."*

*-E.L. Doctorow*

## AUTHOR PLATFORM

Much of your ability to sell nonfiction books comes from your author platform. Author platform is your ability to sell books due to who you are and who you can reach (i.e., because of who you are and what you do). Your nonfiction book, in other words, should be an extension of you and your business. A strong author platform is equally as important, regardless of your method of publishing (e.g., indie, traditional, or a hybrid-approach). Author platform, after all, is what drives readers to your books. And we all want to sell books!

Author platform is not only who you are and what you do, it also extends into other areas such as: social media presence, prior published books, existing readership, personality, previous media experience, and expertise. Brooke Warner of *The Write Life* weighs in, "...**these very factors are why authors with popular blogs and established fan bases get book deals:** because they've proven that they have a cult of personality, and they follow-through."[2] It's not enough to have a strong presence in one area, it takes all of them working together to build your author platform. Of course, we all have to start somewhere and if you're writing your first book, you won't have prior books to add to the foundation of your platform, but you may have videos of Ted Talks or other speaking engagements, you may have blogs and news articles (other sources of writing in your niche) that help to build your platform for your first book. (By the way, author platform comes into play for fiction authors too. However, it generally consists of creating a back list of books).

If you don't have an author platform yet, it can

be overwhelming. Even if you have a small platform and wish to build upon it prior to writing your first book, it is a big challenge. Remember to start small. Take it slow. If you continue writing, speaking, and working/taking action in your niche, you will build your platform organically. But it won't be accomplished overnight. It's a long process, but a worthwhile one. And whenever you're ready to write your book, remember that above everything else if you have a compelling topic to write about and strong writing to back it up, you're well on your way to becoming a nonfiction author.

*"When all else fails, write what your heart tells you. You can't depend on your eyes when your imagination is out of focus."*

*-Mark Twain*

## NICHE

A niche is a distinct segment of the market. Your niche should be something you are passionate about, have experience in, and enjoy. I have several niches (each with their own separate author platforms). I started my author career writing books on animal welfare. As the co-founder and Executive Director of Advocates 4 Animals, Inc. – a 501c3 non-profit animal welfare organization, I had a strong platform. In addition to writing books on animal welfare, I have grown to include books on: writing, motivation, and my fiction niche in love stories. Most authors have at least one niche, as it lets readers know you're an expert in that area. It also lets readers know they can trust you for reliable content in that subject. Author Joanna Penn has two. She writes nonfiction on writing, while she also writes supernatural thrillers (fiction, written under the name J.F. Penn). She's been writing for years in both of her niches and readers know what to expect from her on both fronts. We trust her because she has a back-list, and she has ways we can find her outside of her books (e.g., websites, blogs, podcasts, speaking events). She is clearly dedicated to her two niches.

Once you know your niche, spend time reading the top selling books in that area. What is it about those books that appeals to readers? Read the reviews of those books. What elements of the books resonate with readers? What do the readers wish had been done better? Study the covers of the bestselling books in your niche. What do they have in common? Can your professional cover designer create a similar look for your cover? What keywords are the bestselling authors utilizing in your niche? Don't underestimate the power of keywords (S.E.O. – search engine optimization) and its benefits in helping potential readers find your book.

> *"With a pencil and a piece of paper, I create worlds.*
> *What do you do for a living?"*

## SET GOALS, STAY ON TASK

Whether it's 200 or 5000 words, set a word count goal to keep you on task during your writing sessions. Maybe you find writing time while your children are attending gymnastics class and piano lessons. You can set a word count goal for the day. For example: write 500 words each day. That doesn't mean you must write them all in one sitting. Find creative pockets of time throughout the day where you can add to your body of work. Little sessions of time add up over the long haul. If you don't like the idea of a word count goal, you can set a time goal. For example: write one hour a day. Some days you may achieve it in a non-stop one hour session, others you may grab several twenty-minute writing sessions to reach your goal. The point is, set a daily goal and find creative ways to get there. In a year from now when you have a complete novel, you'll be glad you did.

How will you write each day? Will you carry a notebook and pen? Will you write on a laptop? Will you dictate your novel using Dragon Dictate or another similar program?

For every scene and every chapter you write, ask yourself, why does this matter? How is this adding to the overall story? How is it adding to the readers' experience? And always keep the story interesting. Nonfiction books are filled with statistics. While facts are interesting and important, remember that it's what you bring to the story that makes your book unique. Include stories from your own experiences – lessons learned, obstacles overcome – and what you've learned from interviewing others in the field. There is a delicate balance between stories and statistics and it's important to adhere to that balance when writing your book. No one wants to read a book that's too heavy on one side or the other; they need to seamlessly blend together enough so that we (the reader) forget we're reading (and learning) and we become engrossed in the story being told.

Staying on task can prove especially challenging in our technology driven world. Improve your focus by turning off all distractions during writing time (e.g., turn your phone off or at least put it on airplane mode and keep it out of reach!). You're probably nodding your head right now, it sounds easy enough, right? But it can be tempting. *I'll just check my e-mail, or I just want to Google this one thing…*before we know it we've lost an entire thirty-minutes or an hour, surfing the web instead of writing our book. And then we complain that we never have enough time to write. It can happen so easily, to any of us, on any given day. If, when writing, you have something you need to look up on Google, highlight it and come back to it after your writing session is complete (i.e., word count or time goal has been met). Otherwise, it's too easy to fall victim to the lure of procrastination. Other things you can do to improve your focus during writing time: wear headphones with soft classical music or nature sounds to drown out outside noise. Mark Salzman, author of *True Notebooks* explained that he wore large headphones stuffed with washcloths to drown out the outside noise as he wrote in his home office. Sharing his home with two cats, Mark also read that cats aren't particularly fond of aluminum foil. As much as Mark loved his cats, they always wanted to sit on his lap while he was writing and for him, it was a distraction. So he began making himself an "aluminum foil skirt" to be sure he could stay focused during his dedicated writing time. I can't help but chuckle every time I picture it. But it worked for Mark. What works for you? My favorite writing spot is my home office. My four rescue dogs each have a pet bed to lounge on, toys to play with and bones to chew on while I work. I have a small window, and I always love dreary, rainy days when I'm writing. But if it's sunny and warm outside, if the sidewalks are full of families walking and riding bikes, of children playing basketball in their driveways, the noise can be distracting. I turn on classical music, softly, only so that it drowns out the outside distractions, and I'm able to focus.

I've also found that exercising improves my focus. With daily exercise I'm able to sit still for a period of time and write, instead of constantly fidgeting. It's also helpful to me when writing for a longer period of time, to take a break and walk outside. Just a quarter-mile, if that's all I have time for, will do the trick. I come back to my desk feeling refreshed and renewed, ready to fill blank pages with more breathings of my heart. In addition, like Mark, I can't share my writing space with my foster cats. I love them dearly and spend time with them outside of writing. But when I'm working on a novel, if one of my cats is with me, they are generally climbing on my lap or playfully biting the corner of the computer screen while wobbling my computer back and forth, and it distracts me from my work. Getting to know yourself as a writer will be beneficial to your writing life. When you learn what works for you (and perhaps more importantly, what doesn't), you know how to get the most quality from your writing time. Of course, there will be days when we write easily and others where we stare at the blinking cursor on the computer screen, wondering where all of the stories in our head have gone. But setting specific goals (e.g., word count) and knowing how to create the best writing circumstances for ourselves during the pockets of time we find, will help us become more efficient with our writing, and in turn, increase our quality of writing and level of productivity.

*"Creativity can't be studied or copied. It's a gift."*

## FUNNELS

What is a funnel? It's not a funnel cake. Oh…I loved funnel cakes when I was a kid! My mom would take us to Kings Island (an amusement park in Ohio) in the summer. At the end of a day filled with roller coaster rides, she'd buy us all one funnel cake topped heavy with powdered sugar, to share before heading home. Okay, now my mouth is watering and I have no way of accessing a funnel cake. It looks like a handful of blueberries will have to do for now. But I digress. Funnels are not funnel cakes at all. So, what is a funnel?

A book funnel is anything that leads readers to your books. For example, it might be offering the first book in your series, for free. In this case, authors refer to the free first in series book as the funnel book (hint: if you release your free book in eBook format, rather than print, your costs will dramatically decrease). In theory, if your first (free) book is good, readers will likely buy the rest of the series. Instead of sitting back and hoping readers *might* find you, a new or unknown author, you've created a funnel to lead them to your book without risk or obligation. Step back into your reader shoes. As a reader, it can be difficult to try a new author. We like our tried and trusted authors. We rely on them when we're looking for our next book. *Does Jodi Picoult have a new book? Yes, she does. That's what I'll read.* We tell ourselves this because we want a guarantee that we'll like the book. Therefore, trying a new author – paying for the book and giving them our time and attention – is a lot to ask. It's a wonder any new authors ever find readers! So let's take away the risk. Let's take away some of the fear. Let's make it easy for readers to give us a chance. This is how book funnels work.

Book funnels can be any number of things, not just giving away a first in series book for free. The approach shouldn't be to create a "one-and-done" book funnel, it should be to create as many as possible. We want readers to find our book and give it a chance. To do this, we can create book funnels in any number of places, including but not limited to: guest blog posts, book reviews (have our book reviewed by book bloggers), press releases, our other books (the larger our backlist in a particular topic/genre, the better), other products- such as mugs, T-shirts (hint: utilize print-on-demand services, but always be sure to check the quality first!). We can also create book funnels by offering our book temporarily for sale (e.g., $0.99, one week only). We can be sure our book is published not only as an eBook, but also in paperback, hardback, and as an audiobook. We can be sure our books are published wide. To publish wide means to not be exclusive with one book distributor. The more places your books can be found, the more readers who have the potential to read them.

What funnels have you created for your book (or which ones will you create once your book is published)? By the way, if you're still daydreaming about funnel cakes, you can always enjoy a funnel cake while creating (or brainstorming) your book funnel plans. Why not? Writing is hard work. We need to enjoy ourselves too!

> *"We artists are a different breed of people. We're a happy bunch."*
>
> *-Bob Ross*

## PROFESSIONALS

As has been touched on throughout the book, working with professionals in a must. You are a professional writer. In order to be a professional at your job, it's important to collaborate with other professionals to create a quality product. Find beta-readers in your target market. This can be difficult when you're first starting, but don't allow yourself to become discouraged. Keep searching. Your beta-readers are out there and once you find them, hang on tight. The key is to find honest beta-readers who enjoy the topic you're writing about. If you find someone to beta-read your nonfiction book on long-distance running, and while they love to read, they've never been much for exercise, you haven't found your target beta-reader. Not only do you want to find beta-readers who are in your target market (i.e., those enjoy your topic, and who read other books on the topic, outside of yours), you want to find as many beta-readers as you can. The more eyes you can have on your book prior to sending it off to the editor(s), the better. Creating a question sheet can be helpful for feedback from the beta-readers. Some readers, while they love to read, find it hard to give feedback, especially to an author they may know. Providing them with direct questions up front can help early readers provide you with useful feedback.

Once you've edited your book yourself and gotten feedback from as many beta-readers as possible (and made corrections, updates, etc.), it's time to send your book to the editor. Working with a professional editor is imperative to your success. I've met many young authors who have chosen to bypass the editing process on their first book, to spare themselves the expense. This choice is often a set up for failure. If they find readers, once published, readers are quick to note in the reviews that the book needs to be edited. They are also quick to erase the author from their mind (or worse, tell others to be sure *not* to read their books). You don't want to be *this* author. You want to have a quality, professional product. You want to build a solid foundation for yourself. This is your writing life, make the most of it. Present yourself as a professional and your readers will thank you with referrals to other eager readers, and with purchases of your future books.

Finding the right editor is much like dating. It's tough. And even once you find *the one*, receiving feedback can be brutal. But an editor's job is to help you be the best writer you can be. They assist in making books clean, clear, and easy to read. Once you've survived the editing process, it's time to send the book off to your proofreader (the final edit before publication). Again, it's not always easy to find a well-matched proofreader, but when you do, hang on to them. Like our editors, proofreaders make our work the best it can be. They make sure our words shine. They make sure we don't get any negative reviews based on spelling or punctuation errors. They are there to help us.

As a side note, I run a book blog (*www.StaceysBookBlog.com*) and I'm inundated with book review inquiries each month. I love running the blog and of course, I love reading books (especially when I've discovered an author new to me!). By reading a quick sample of the proposed book, I can always tell whether or not a book has been professionally edited. If it has not, I will not agree to review the book. There is a lot of competition in the book market- across every genre and topic area – and I want to spend my time reading books that, at the very least, have been professionally edited.

In what seems like a lifetime ago, I was a Realtor. When I showed houses to buyers, I knew within the first ten-seconds of walking into a house if the buyer would be interested in it or not. If the house was dark (e.g., curtains closed, lights off), if there was a stain on the carpet, if the chairs weren't neatly tucked in at the kitchen table, I would watch as the buyers wrinkled their noses and told me they didn't need to see anymore. They would practically run out the door. On the other hand, if I walked into a home with buyers and the curtains were drawn back, allowing natural light to flood into the rooms, if all of the lights were turned on, the house was clean and smelled nice, the buyers always wanted the full tour. They wanted to give the house a chance (even if it wasn't the perfect layout or a big enough backyard). They were willing to do a full walk-through because of the way the house was presented. It was obvious that the owner put great care into their home. It was inviting; welcoming. The same holds true for books. In a sense, you are the Realtor of your book. There are plenty of potential buyers out there, but you have to give them a reason to want to take a chance on you. Like the buyers who walked into the unkempt, unwelcoming houses, so too are the books which have not been edited, nor have a professional cover design. But the houses that had their lights turned on, the ones that were spotlessly clean and smelled like a fresh burning candle, the houses that seemed to say: "Please, come in! We love it here and we know you will too!" They were in demand and sold because of their presentation. Houses are no different than books that present themselves in this manner. When we become the Realtor of our book, we invite readers in. We make it comfortable and easy for readers to give us a chance. But in order to accomplish this, we must be professionals and we must work collaboratively with other professionals to produce our best product.

Another professional we need to work with is a cover designer. Unless your day job is as a professional photographer/graphic designer, do not attempt to design your own cover. It will show. When I am pitched for book reviews on my blog, one of the first things I do is look at the book cover. Is it appealing? It is professionally done? It is appropriate for the topic/genre? Covers are one of our biggest marketing tools. I don't know about you, but I always remember book covers. I sometimes forget specific titles, but the covers I can describe down to the last detail. There are times when I'm reading, and I'll flip back to the cover ponder the story being told between the covers. Maybe that's weird, but I've done it since I was a kid. I've been fascinated with book covers for as long as I can remember. Ask yourself, what does your cover say about your book? Is it similar to other books in your genre? Is it professionally done? Even so, does it *look* professional? Much like with the beta-readers you work with early on the path-to-publication process, you can ask a large (the greater the number, the better) number of people, their impressions of your potential book cover. You can have a selection of three potential cover designs from your designer, and ask for feedback on social media. Allow your readers to vote on the cover they like best for your next book (this is also a great way to gain early interest in your next book!). Some programs, such as *99designs.com* offer you a choice between multiple cover design options. You choose a design you love or receive a money back guarantee. Remember, readers will often study your cover before reading the bio of your book. Make it a good one. Work with a professional to create a cover that reflects the look and feel of your topic. Be the Realtor of your book. Presentation matters. Of course, we have to have written a good story. But barring that we've done our job as writing professionals, let's collaborate with professionals in their areas of expertise to package our product in the best way possible. Let's welcome readers to our book with a great cover. Let's keep them reading with stellar editing. And let's keep them coming back for more of our books, by giving them a great story.

*"What if is always a good start for story ideas."*

*-Lois Lowry, author of The Giver*

## WHAT'S IT ABOUT?

When someone inevitably asks you about your book, they will likely say "What's it about?" Translation: *Would I like the book? Is it worth the investment of my time and money?* We discussed the same question in the previous chapter on fiction. You will be asked this question and you must be prepared with an answer. And the faster you can deliver the answer, the better.

The more compelling your words, the more effective your answer. You don't want to stumble when given a chance to tell a potential reader about your book. Prepare an honest, alluring answer that you can deliver in under thirty-seconds (bonus points for twenty-seconds or less). With nonfiction books, the answer is often included in the title. Here's an example: for my book, *Covered in Pet Fur: How to Start an Animal Rescue, The Right Way*, I answer the question with this: "It's a book for anyone interested in starting or volunteering for an animal rescue. It's a *how-to* mixed with our experiences and stories from over a decade in the field." This answer, and the book itself, have proven to be appealing to the right market. Those who love animals and want to learn more about starting a rescue (or volunteering for one), pick up the book and provide positive feedback. Those who are not interested in this topic, move on.

Nonfiction authors have a lot to compete with. Not only other books on the same topic, but there are free blogs, videos, and articles that are easy to access. Why should readers choose to spend their money and time with *your* book over all the other options? Another way to ask this question is to ask why you're writing a book on a topic that's already been covered many times before, by many other writers. The answer is because of what *you* bring to it. The answer is, because of *you*. Remember it's not only who you are (e.g., personality, presence) but also your experiences (i.e., why you're an expert in the field). This is why a reader buys your book. You are unique and because of that, a reader wants to experience (and learn about) a topic from your perspective.

> *"To write something you have to risk making a fool of yourself."*
>
> *-Anne Rice*

## HOW TO AVOID COMMON MISTAKES IN NONFICTION WRITING

- Proofread. Proofread. Proofread.

- Hire a professional editor.

- Land as many eyes on your book (beta-readers) and as much feedback as you can prior to publication.

- Don't present only facts and figures. Share personal experiences, research, interviews and stories.

- Have a clever book title (and one that lets

us know what your book is about).

- Hook the reader from the first sentence.

- Utilize humor when possible.

- Don't be afraid to be vulnerable. Vulnerability makes you relatable.

- Let us know (on the cover and in the book write-up) what we can expect to learn from reading your book.

- Let us know why you're an expert and what makes you uniquely qualified to teach us about this topic.

- Hire a professional cover designer.

- Be able to state what your book is about, in thirty-seconds or less (i.e., Is it compelling? Will we learn something interesting and/or helpful?).

- Provide opportunities for readers to find you (in your niche) outside of your book (e.g., other books, speaking events, videos, podcasts, blogs, etc.).

- Understand your reader (what do they want to learn/know?).

# Editors

*"The difference between the almost right word and the right word is really a large matter—it's the difference between the lightning bug and the lightning."*

*-Mark Twain*

Three wise pieces of advice on editing your book:

- When in doubt, *cut it out.*
- Mark Twain said something along the lines of…Replace every *"very"* with *"damn".*

Your editor will remove either word anyway.

- Work with a professional editor.

First things first, of course. Write the book. You won't have anything to be edited without writing the story. Once the book is written, distance yourself from it before looking at it again. For me, I generally like to stay away from my book for at least two weeks before revisiting it. At that point I read my entire body of work from start to finish. I self-edit. I do three read-throughs. One, to be sure the story makes sense (e.g., one scene builds to the next, pace, character consistency, overall impact of the story). The second, to search for technical errors (e.g., spelling, word order, long sentences, paragraph breaks). And the third, to reword passive voice. Readers appreciate confidence and prefer an active rather than a passive voice. "Writers try to avoid the passive voice when possible because the passive voice often leads to wordier and less powerful sentences. Instead, writers prefer the active voice because the subject of the sentence is actually doing the action (thus making the sentence more commanding and confident)."[1] Example, below:

181

- Passive voice: *"The midterm exams were graded by the instructor."*

- Active voice: *"The instructor graded the midterm exams."*

Often, I read out loud on the third self-edit, to be sure the words flow smoothly. If I stumble while reading, it often means the sentence, paragraph, or scene need reworked. In addition, it is helpful to utilize a grammar website (e.g., *grammarly.com, the Hemingway App*) to check for additional errors. After the pre-check of self-edits, it's time to work with beta-readers. Beta-readers should be readers who regularly read in your genre or topic. Provide a questionnaire to prompt beta-readers to provide useful feedback. The more beta-readers you have, the better (aim for a minimum of three). You want as many eyeballs on your book before sending it off to the editor. While you can certainly have your mom or sister be a beta-reader for your book, be sure to include readers outside of your family and friends. Beta-reading is an important step in the process. You are looking for honest feedback that will serve to help strengthen your book. Of course, you may not agree with every comment every beta-reader provides. However, there will likely be common themes to what your beta-readers point out. If nearly every beta-reader confides that the story's pace is too slow, this is something you do not want to ignore.

Once you've completed your self-edits, read your work out loud, replaced passive voice with active voice, made sure the pace and order of your story are up to par, utilized a grammar website, spell checked, and received helpful feedback from your beta-readers, it's time to work with your professional editor. You will also want to professionally format your book. Depending on your editor, you may choose to do this before or after this step. Keep in mind, formatting your book for paperback requires a separate process from formatting your eBook (Hint: professional programs such as Vellum are helpful). If you try to format the books yourself, understand that when you forgo a professional service, the quality of your product may suffer. In today's ever-changing world of eReaders, our formatting often appears different on each reader (e.g., iPhone reading app vs. an eReader device). When working with a professional service, they will format your book to coordinate properly with the growing number of eReader devices.

> *"Books aren't written– they're re-written. Including your own. It is one of the hardest things to accept, especially after the seventh rewrite hasn't quite done it."*

> *-Michael Crichton*

Patience is one of the most important aspects of the editing process. When writing a book, I go through various stages of "This will be the greatest book ever written!" to "I've spent so much time writing this, what if my editor hates it?" However, when I reach the editing process, the project becomes a different beast. I've read countless books and articles that tell writers to embrace the editing process. But for me, it's excruciating. Admittedly, I'm getting better, after having ten published books. Nevertheless, it's still a painful process. I worry that my book isn't good enough. I nearly melt at the sight of countless red marks donning every page. I convince myself I'll never publish the book, that I'm too overwhelmed, that my writing isn't as good as someone else's (falling victim to comparitinitis). Even after I've read through the edits and re-written my story, I doubt myself as I send it off to editor number two. Will my book survive this round of edits? I worry. And once again, the book, no matter how much I believe in its story, no matter how perfect I think it is (that point when I feel that there's no way someone can find another error or anything to change), comes back covered in red marks, ready for another round of re-writes.

It is all part of the process. I often compare it to painting a room. I like to paint. And I love the look of a freshly painted area. When we think about repainting a room, we think of what color we'll paint it. We think of laughing and listening to music as we paint the walls with a friend. We think of how great the room will look when it's complete. However, we often forget to think about preparing to paint (e.g., taping off the trim, placing tarps down to spare the furniture and floor from runaway drips) and cleaning up (e.g., washing the brushes, recycling unused paint, cleaning any spills and drips). We often fail to think about the length of time it will truly take to paint the entire room. The same holds true with writing a book. We have a story burning inside of us that we're ready to share. We love to write. We can't wait to hold the finished product in our hands. We can't wait to see our book selling more and more copies each day. But we often forget about the nitty gritty. The self-editing. The grammar checks. The reading out loud. The beta-readers. The professional editors. The final proofreader. And because we forget (or don't want) to think about these crucial elements, we quickly grow impatient when we get there. We want to rush through the "boring stuff". We want to minimize its importance. But doing that will only serve to negatively impact our final product. If we want a professional, well-packaged product, we need to slow down, take a deep breath and learn to embrace the process. Admittedly, the editing process can be grueling. If you're a writer, you understand that every part of the process is demanding. The outlining. The writing. The self-editing. The professional editing. The formatting. The professional cover design. The marketing. The reviews. Every step of the way is taxing. That's why we must love what we're doing. We must love the craft of writing. And if we love it, love allows us to embrace every aspect of the deal. It allows us to understand the importance of every step.

Now that we understand that editing takes patience and it's a necessary element when publishing a book, what is it that editors want writers to know? Kristen Kiefer's blog, *She's Novel* posted a blog on the very topic, written by writing coach and editor Sarah Fox.[2] Fox's list of seven things editors wish writers knew, include:

- Book editors in advance (*editors are often booked months in advance*).

- Factor professional editors into your book budget (*Yes, you need a book budget regardless of how you publish your book- traditional, indie, or a hybrid approach. Editors cost hundreds to thousands of dollars. They spend countless hours polishing your work to be sure it is received well by readers*).

- Understand the different types of editors (*more on this in the following paragraphs*).

- Hire an editor with expertise in your genre (*editors typically do not cover every genre. Hire an editor who works specifically in your genre and understands the market*).

- Pre-edit (self-edit) your book prior to sending it off to an editor (*this will enable an editor to give you the best feedback possible*).

- Don't panic when you see your book heavily marked up (*this is an editor's job! You want your editor to do their job so your book can be at its best*).

- Patience (*editing takes a long time! In my*

*experience, it always takes longer than you think it will- even if you budget a lot of time. Editor Sarah Fox shared: "I wish revising a novel were a short process. I really do. Sadly, that is not the case. It inevitably takes longer than expected. For example, after I did a developmental edit for a client, she realized that she needed another character's point of view in her novel (essentially doubling her manuscript). This added almost a year to her schedule. While this is an extreme case, be prepared for a lengthy revision process. Double the length of time you think it will take for revisions when you prepare your publishing schedule).*

Jen Blood shared the three common issues she finds as an editor.[3] Knowing the most common issues editors encounter, we can pay attention as we work in the self-editing phase (and try to avoid or correct them before our work reaches our editors!).

- "Structural issues like plot holes, wandering timelines, and lagging pace").

- "Excessive exposition or lengthy chunks of narrative (telling vs. showing)".

- "Awkward, clunky writing".

Viewing the lack of white space on a page can assist in locating "lengthy chunks" in your story. A lack of white space indicates a lack of dialogue. It also indicates a lack of paragraph breaks. When your pages lack white space, pay special attention and search for lengthy, muddy sentences (i.e., too wordy!). Reading your book out loud can also help you spot all three of the above issues early in the editing process.

> *"Writing is the painting of the voice."*
>
> *-Voltaire*

There are three general types of editing:

- Developmental or Content editing (*focuses on plot holes, pace, character development*).

- Copyediting (*focuses on details such as*

sentence structure, basic fact checking, consistent style).

- Line editing (*focuses on punctuation, grammatical errors, and typos*). This can also be lumped with Proofreading (*a proofreader is your final editor, making sure every comma is in place, etc.*).

Of editing, thriller author J.F. Penn explains: "Finding an editor is a bit like dating – you have to try a number before you find someone who is the best match. I've been through a number of editors in the last few years, and I'm thrilled to now be working with Jen Blood, who is a brilliant editor but also writes the same type of thrillers as I do. She gets my style of writing, and she understands my violent streak and doesn't try to rein in what makes me me. What she does do is help me to craft a better book by suggesting structural changes and then doing detailed line edits. Jen is my type of editor – of course, that doesn't necessarily make her the right person for you!"[4] Finding the right editor for you is a process. I know, editing is already a process in and of itself. But finding the *best* editor for your books is crucial to the overall success. A good place to start is to look for an editor who specializes in your genre or topic area.

Again, regardless of how you choose to publish your book (traditional, indie, or a hybrid approach), you need a professional editor in your corner. Once you find a handful of editors who specify in your genre and who, after reviewing their website, you feel you may work well with, contact them. While they are incredibly busy, editors should reply to your inquiry within several days. Many editors will offer a free sample of their editing services (e.g., for the first ten pages of your novel) or may offer to edit the first chapter of your book for a small fee (e.g., $30). Once you've gotten to this point, here are few things to consider before hiring your editor:

- Did they provide you with a small, free sample edit?

- Did they provide helpful/useful edits (in the sample)?

- Are they able to meet your timeline?

- Did they respond to your email inquiry in a timely and professional manner?

- Did they send your sample edits within the time frame promised?

- Are the editors' comments and corrections valid? What is their reasoning for the changes?

- Does the editor seem enthusiastic about their work?

- Have they provided you with examples of other books in your genre, which they've edited (and are those books reviewed well online? Are the books legitimately published? Has the editor written published articles on editing)?

- Have you viewed their Resume or CV (this should be available on their website)?

- Have they provided you with a list of references and have you contacted them?

- Are they an independent editor (not third-party)?

- Are they a member of the Editorial Freelancers Association (US), the Society of Freelance Editors and Proofreaders (UK), the Institute of Professional Editors (Australia), or the Editors Association of

Canada?

- What is the cost? Do they offer a deluxe package (that includes multiple types of editing)?

- Does the cost cover a one-time read-through or does it also cover revisions (a second read through)? Be clear up front what the cost covers. Be sure your agreement is clear and in writing.

The cost of hiring an editor can be expensive. However, a professionally edited novel will likely earn you more book sales (and therefore, more money) in the long run (e.g., due to positive reviews, word-of-mouth recommendations, etc.). Likely your book will not succeed if left unedited. Readers are quick to leave reviews commenting on poorly edited (or unedited) books, therefore stifling future readers from giving your book a try. You can write the most intriguing story possible, however if your book is in dire need of edits, readers will become quickly discouraged.

If you absolutely cannot afford a professional editor, there are always creative ways around this.

However, you must understand the type of edits a professional editor provides and the value it gives to your book. When you understand this, you can seek creative solutions. Victoria Strauss of *Writer Beware* explains: "…paid editing is not a magic fix…Even the most accomplished editor can't turn a bad manuscript into a good one. They can only work with what's already there."[5] If you cannot afford a professional editor, first, be sure to self-edit your book (many times!). Do know that self-editing is not enough; you need more eyes on your book (hint: two books I highly recommend before you begin the self-editing process are: *Self Editing for Fiction Writers* by Renni Browne and Dave King, and *Write Right! A Desktop Digest of Punctuation, Grammar, and Style* by Jan Venolia). Next, find beta-readers within your topic or genre. This is a non-negotiable. Where can you find beta-readers? If you're in a writing group, offer to beta-read for each other. If you're a member of a book club, ask other members to participate. Remember, the more beta-readers you have, the better. You want as many eyes as possible on your book. And if you cannot afford a professional editor, put on your creative cap. Visit a local university and ask writing students to edit your novel. Ask professors, too. Ask around among online writer groups (e.g., Critter Writers Workshop for Science Fiction/Fantasy/Horror writers). There are also creative ways to earn extra money to pay for an editor (e.g., aluminum recycling, childcare, pet-sitting). Joanna Penn adds: "Hiring a qualified editor means the difference between you limping across the finish line or soaring past the competition." It cannot be stressed enough, professional editing matters (remember, be a reader first! You would likely not continue reading an unedited or poorly edited book. If you're finding error after error on the page, you'll put the book down and move on to the next one. You don't want this to be *your* book!).

An editor's job is to make your work better. It can be hard to swallow when your manuscript is returned to you, covered in marks. Don't let yourself become overwhelmed (I am saying this to remind myself!). Your editor is there to help you. When you find the right editor for your book, let it be someone you can trust (i.e., cares about your work, meets deadlines). In my own experience, when my edits come back, I like to look them over and wait a day before I begin to digest them. My first look over is quick, allowing me an understanding of the basic feedback I am receiving. One of my first fiction novels was littered with the passive words "tend to" and "seem to". Ouch! As much as it hurt to see my error (that became obvious once my editor pointed it out), I was grateful to know upfront, before my book went into the hands of readers. And it taught me to pay attention to this particular point in my future writing. I realized I had to work on overcoming my passive voice. This was a good thing and has only served to strengthen my writing in the years that have followed. The next day (after I've given myself a day to do a quick glance and absorb some of the shell shock that inevitably comes from the number of corrections awaiting my attention) I read through the edits carefully. I'm now ready to study and to learn from them. Following this read through, I begin implementing the edits and rewriting as needed. I've learned, for me, it helps to take frequent breaks while inputting edits and rewriting. I become so intensely focused on the computer screen, my eyes grow weary from the strain. Tension headaches are not uncommon for me during this phase. I take it chapter by chapter. Sometimes page by page (depending on how brutal the edits are in this round!). I set a goal (e.g., edit/re-write the first two chapters) and then head out on a walk (even if it is midnight). The walk clears my head, gives my eyes a breather from so much focus and renews me with a bout of energy for continuing my edits. Before I started taking walks mid-edit/rewriting, I was incredibly stressed during this process. But as I stated earlier, I've learned to go with the flow. It's part of the magic that creates a published book. It's part of what takes a book from good to great. So, the way I see it, learning to accept the editing process for what it is (grueling, tedious, overwhelming) is our best bet.

Editors matter. Yes, they can be expensive. Yes, the process will take double (or more) time than you expect. Yes, it can bring you to tears. Yes, it can give you tension headaches. Yes, you will likely be sick of your story (the story you believe in and love!) by the time your book is edited, polished, and published. But it's part of the magic. It's part of the journey. Writing is hard. No one ever said it was easy. But you're a writer. You can write your novel. You can make it to the glorious words of THE END. And you can survive the editing process. You can do this!

When I receive submissions to my book blog, it is evident within the first chapter (often within the first two pages) if a book has been professionally edited. If it has not, I lose interest in the story quickly. I read a lot of books and want to spend my time with books that have been handled with professionalism and great care. I assume you do, too. We want to find readers who read a lot of books, too. After all, they're our ideal consumers. If they read a lot of books and they like ours, they'll buy our backlist. They'll buy our new releases. They'll leave positive reviews. They'll recommend our books to other readers. If this is what we want, we need to take proper care when handling our product. We need to be sure it is professionally edited and polished before sending it off to our agent, publisher, or readers. We need to be sure it is our best work. Remember, presentation matters. Like a Realtor showing a house, I know when reviewing a book for my book blog, the books that will sell well and those that won't. As a former Realtor, I knew every time I took buyers into a home, if they would be interested or if they wanted to sprint back to their cars and move on to the next option. It's no different with a book. What scared home buyers was when sellers left their homes dark and unkempt. What scares book buyers is no different. We don't want to read an unprofessional, unedited book. Home buyers want to walk into a house that is well-lit, clean, and welcoming. Book readers want the same thing. We want to look at a book with a professional cover. We want to read a title and tag line that pull us in. We want to open the novel and see a professionally formatted and edited book.

Presentation matters. Make your book the best it can be.

## 9

## How to Market Your Book

*"It's like a fingerprint or singing voice. There's something that belongs to you that just gets into your writing…"*

*-Lorrie Moore*

Throughout the years I've interviewed countless authors in a wide array of genres. I've conducted author interviews for local newspapers and I continue to interview authors now on my book blog. I've been fascinated with authors for as long as I can remember. It only seems like yesterday when author R.L. Stine came to visit our middle school. I was in awe. I'd read every book he'd written. I was a huge fan, and he came to talk to *our* school! The same school year I was one of ten students to win a pizza selling contest. Our prize was to ride in a limousine and go out to eat (for pizza, no less). While I found the limo ride fun, listening to a published author speak proved more thrilling. I'm fascinated with creative entrepreneurs. How did they get to where they are? Did they always know they wanted to be a writer? What was their break-through moment? Every facet of the author interview enthralls me. In addition to being enamored with the interviews, I've learned (and continue to learn) a lot. And what authors tell me, repeatedly, is the number one aspect they most dislike in the writing process? Surprisingly it isn't the editing process. Okay, you guessed it, it's the title of this chapter: marketing. Many authors despise marketing. Regardless of how you're published (indie, traditional, hybrid), marketing is essential, and it's up to you. We are all author entrepreneurs, in fact. And part of being a successful entrepreneur is marketing. Funny enough, one of the top questions I'm asked as an author is: "How do I market my book?" And "What can I do to market my book without the cost?"

What is marketing, really? Marketing is getting the word out, letting the world know about your book (beyond answering the question, "what is your book about?"). Marketing is letting readers in your target market know that your book is available- and that it's good! This means you have to know *who* your target market is and where to find them. Overwhelmed yet? Stick with me.

My first published fiction book was a novella (a love story), *The First and Last Everything*. At the time, I had five published nonfiction books. All of my nonfiction books were focused on animal welfare. I'd spent more than a decade as the co-founder and Executive Director of a 501c3 non-profit animal welfare organization, *Advocates 4 Animals, Inc.* (and many more years volunteering at shelters across the country). I had branded myself in this area. The book I co-wrote with our organizations co-founder became a bestseller, gaining attention from RIVA media and Animal Planet. So, publishing fiction – a love story – was new territory for me. It was way out of my brand.

Upon publication of *The First and Last Everything*, outside of the sales from my friends, family, and colleagues, I sold less than 10 copies. Admittedly, the book had zero marketing. Zilch. I'd simply crossed my fingers, priced low, and hoped. Not exactly the wisest strategy (if it's not clear, I do not recommend this as a successful marketing plan). I was incredibly nervous. Because of my deviation from what I was known for – animal welfare – I worried that I'd have crossover readers who would expect the book to include animal rescue elements (it doesn't). I worried that they would think I was strange for writing love stories. I was known as a leader in the animal rescue community, not a romance novelist. In short, I was unsure of myself (albeit I was writing fiction under a pen name at the time. I've since ditched the pen name and all of my books are now published under my given name). A week after my fiction book's publication, however, I went to an appointment at a new hair salon. My stylist asked what I did for a living. I told her I was the director of a non-profit and a writer. At the word *writer,* another stylist perked up and asked if I'd written any books. She said she was an avid reader and wound up buying my book on her eReader, on the spot (thank goodness I had my "what is the book about?" reply prepared!). I consider myself lucky to have met one of my first fiction fans face to face (a rare occurrence in today's technology driven society). It was an amazing experience. I admit, I was flattered (and for a moment, my face was red, too. I worried I was doing something wrong by "selling myself"). And so it began. My fiction book began to sell by word of mouth. Other stylists read the book. They shared it on their social media pages and with clients. Awhile later, my book went on sale and boosted sales again. I began adding another layer to my brand (i.e., to what I represent). And I wrote two more fiction novels, adding to my backlist (and those first readers faithfully and eagerly bought my next books, too). With each new book, I continued to gain more readers.

I've learned about marketing from my interviews with other authors, my entrepreneur and business marketing background, and from good old trial and error (however, what works in one industry may differ from another). I hadn't meant to market myself that day in the hair salon, but it happened. It was uncomfortable. I worried that my book wasn't good enough. But I was vulnerable. And I gained loyal readers. How can you gain readers outside of chance encounters in hair salons? There are plenty of ways and we're going to dive into them now.

*"People do not buy goods and services. They buy relations, stories and magic."*

*-Seth Godin*

## FREE AND LOW-COST MARKETING IDEAS FOR YOUR BOOK

Not all marketing efforts are equal. Not all marketing efforts yield direct results, either (meaning when you do X, it does not guarantee to translate to a specific number of book sales). Marketing efforts are not a one-and-done deal. To be successful, marketing efforts should be ongoing and varied. The combination of marketing efforts that work best for one author, may be a flop for another. Knowing *who* your potential readers are is helpful. Below, we dive into a number of free and low-cost marketing ideas for your book. Try each method more than once. Be consistent. In time, you'll find your winning combination as you watch your book sales climb.

### Guest Blog

You don't have to have your own blog to spread the word about your latest book. Being a guest blogger on a high traffic blog is a great way to gain interest from potential new readers. Be sure to seek blogs that offer articles on a topic relevant to your book(s). If you write books on motivation and inspiration, find blogs that aim to offer this type of information to their readers. In addition, before pitching your idea, be sure to read the guidelines for guest bloggers. Don't write an article *about* your book. Rather, choose an aspect of your book, write on that topic, and mention your book title and website in the two-line bio at the end. If readers find your blog post intriguing, they may glance at your bio and click on the link to your book.

## Guest on T.V., Radio, or other Local Media Source

Connect with your local television or radio stations. What creative opportunities are available? Utilize these mediums much like a guest blogger. This can work especially well for nonfiction books. Let them know why you are an expert in your field and what you can bring to their show (e.g., teaching viewers/listeners how to use positive reinforcement dog training). Be flexible with time schedules (the show may need to fill a canceled time slot with last minute notice- this could be your opportunity!).

## Support a Local Non-profit

This is a great way to support a local cause you believe in and to reach potential new readers. Offer to donate 20% of all book sale proceeds in the month of May, to your favorite charity. Let the charity know in advance (and encourage them to share a flyer and website link on their social media pages).

## Giveaways & Contests

Generate interest in your book by offering a giveaway or contest. On my website (*www.StaceyRitzBooks.com*) I offer a free monthly book giveaway. I giveaway free audiobooks, print books, and eBooks. Each month a different giveaway is provided and anyone currently signed up for my newsletter is eligible to win.

## Website

Have a professional, easy to navigate author website. The website should clearly state who you are and where to find your books. Although a website won't necessarily bring more readers, it will serve to provide those considering (or currently) reading your book(s), a spot to find more information about you (and your backlist of books). Building a connection with your readers can go a long way. Readers who feel they know you are more likely to leave reviews, recommend your books to others, and buy your next books. Your website should be clean and uncluttered. It should be clear to the visitor within seconds what type of books you write. The site should be credible, easy to navigate, provide links to your bio, and to your books. Professional author websites also serve many other purposes such as: media kit/press page, another place for readers to find and buy your books (outside of big retailers), options for readers to purchase autographed copies of your print books, newsletter sign-up, and more.

## E-mail List & Newsletter

Start with one subscriber! Your writing career is a business. Remember, you are the entrepreneur of your writing life. When starting your email newsletter list, likely you will start with one subscriber (or at least one subscriber outside of your friends, family, and co-workers). It is hard to press send when you have one subscriber. Believe me, I've been there. In my personal experience, I felt embarrassed. Why was I spending so much time putting together a professional newsletter for one person? I felt like a fool. But I pressed on, knowing I would gain additional subscribers in the coming months and years. The hard work and effort you put into your email list and newsletter are worth it. Be sure to only send the newsletter to individuals who choose to subscribe to your list and always offer an unsubscribe button within the text. The last thing you want to do is continue to send e-mails to someone who doesn't want to receive your emails (you will not gain a reader this way, you will only become annoying).

Look at the long-term sustainability of your writing career. An email list is helpful because, unlike the myriad of ever changing social media platforms, you have control of your email list. Once upon a time, everyone saw everyone's Facebook posts in their feed. Today, however, the platform has changed, allowing a shrinking percentage of your followers to ever see your posts (unless you buy ads). An email list, on the other hand, provides you with direct contact to your readers. No matter what changes social media platforms implement in the future, your email list is yours.

Be sure to treat your email list with respect. Do not over send emails, at the risk of readers becoming overwhelmed and simply hitting delete. Provide helpful, interesting information within the context of your newsletter. And stick to a schedule. Do you send a newsletter every Monday? Once a month? Twice a month? Create a schedule and stick to it. Let your readers know what they can expect and be consistent.

## Go Wide

It can be tempting to sell exclusively with one book distributor (when being offered a larger percentage of pay on each book sale). However, going wide has many benefits. Going wide, or expanded distribution means offering your book for sale in as many places as possible. Why consider this route? The more places your books can be found, the more potential readers you can reach. In addition, if you list your book for sale with only one distributor, what happens if that distributor changes the rules or goes out of business? Your readers won't know where to find you. Every author's strategy is different and you must choose the best route for you, given the point where you are in your writing career. If you have one published book it may serve you best to go exclusive with one distributor until you build up a backlist of books. Book distributor rules are ever changing. Do your research and make the best decision for yourself and continue to revisit your decision in the coming months and years. Research and study the market before deciding what is best for your long-term sustainability as a writer.

## Intriguing Story

This should go without saying. Write an intriguing story! The first chapter sells the book (i.e., if someone reads a free sample of your book online, likely if your first chapter is good, they'll purchase the book). The last chapter (and the overall feeling the reader is left with at the end of your book) is what sells your next book. Working with beta-readers after completing your first several drafts, and before your book heads to the editor, can help shape and form your story into one that is compelling and interesting to readers in your genre.

## Reviews

When I ask authors what they dislike most about marketing, most of them tell me: "asking for reviews." And I totally agree. Asking for reviews is uncomfortable. Not only are we asking a stranger to read our book (often that means they are taking a chance on a new author), we are asking them to then go online and write a review about what they've read.

But it's something all authors need to do. When we ask our readers for reviews we take a risk. No matter how polished and compelling our story is, we may receive a bad review and this is out of our control. We can ask for readers to leave reviews, but we have no idea how our book will impact them. As mentioned earlier, every reader brings a different and unique set of experiences and ideas with them before sitting down to read. This means a book will potentially create a different reaction from every reader. Do not ask for reviews from family members. Rather, ask your newsletter subscribers, your writing group, your social media followers, and post a note in the back of your book asking readers to take a moment to leave a review before picking up their next book.

Honest reviews are helpful to potential readers. They let readers know what the story is about. They also let potential readers know if the book is edited, formatted properly, and if the writer provides a compelling story. Was the pace lagging or was the book a page-turner?

**Write More Books**

Typically, once you have five (or more) books in a specific genre, you will begin to see an increase in sales. Sadly, many published authors end their careers once they've reached just two or three books. They leave the industry wondering why their books never sold.

We live in a day and age of Netflix binging. When we watch or read something, we want to know that there is more. If we choose a new television series to watch we generally check to see how many seasons are available before committing ourselves to the show. Similarly, many readers express their preference to read established authors with big backlists. Why? Because they know if they enjoy the book, there are plenty more just like it that they can savor. Traditionally, the larger your backlist, the more potential you have at hooking new readers (readers who will be likely to buy your other books).

## Intellectual Property Assets

Your book is an intellectual property asset. What does this mean? An intellectual property asset is something that will continue to earn money for you over time. When jump starting your writing career and working to create a long-term sustainable income through writing, realizing that books are intellectual property assets can transform your author business.

Intellectual property assets can create scalable income. Scalable income is when you create something once, that can be sold again and again (e.g., a book. You write and collaborate with other professionals to publish your book. Once published, your book can sell forever. You don't have to rewrite the book for every unique sale). They key to success with intellectual property assets, such as books, is to continue creating them. Build your backlist. What else can you do? Turn your manuscript into various products: print books, eBooks, and audiobooks. The more products you can create from your book, the more potential you have to raise your scalable income.

## Social Media

There are an ever-growing number of social media platforms to choose from. Some authors take the approach of being active on every social media page. Others focus on one or two platforms and work to grow their audience there. You are the C.E.O. of your writing life. Which combination of social media platforms will you choose? Social media platforms are generally free and provide another way for your readers (*and* potential new readers) to find you and to get to know you and your style/tone/personality. You can also utilize social media to ask for opinions. If you've narrowed your choice of book covers from your designer down to two, post them both on social media and ask followers to vote on which cover they like the best. Not only does this draw interest to your upcoming book, it allows people to feel involved in the process, likely enhancing their connection to you.

## Book Signings & Events

While book signings may seem to be a thing of the past, they can still prove useful in today's world, if done correctly. Knowing your potential readers can be especially helpful when coordinating a book signing event. I held a book signing for my animal welfare books in conjunction with our non-profit fundraising event at Barnes & Noble. A portion of all proceeds from my animal welfare books are donated to life-saving efforts at Advocates 4 Animals and holding the two events together proved successful. In addition, I've held book signings at other Advocates 4 Animals fundraisers such as our annual Silent Auction. When holding a book signing, look to where your potential readers are gathering. Place yourself among readers who are likely to read your topic/genre of books.

## Speaking

Look for speaking opportunities in your area of focus and expertise. If you write books on writing, speak at writer's retreats and to genre specific groups. Whatever your topic, search for ways to speak about it. Much like guest blogging, you don't want to speak specifically on your book. No one wants to listen to a writer speak about his book. Rather, we want to hear him speak about how he became a writer. Or if he writes books on animal welfare, we want to hear about his experiences in the field. The fact that you have a book is a bonus and should be included in the short bio provided on the website or handouts at the event. Bring print copies of your book to offer for sale following the event. Bring business cards with your website and book title included. Speaking can be done in front of a live audience (e.g., Ted Talk, visiting a school) or can be done on video (e.g., YouTube). Speaking opportunities are another way for your readers (and potential new readers) to get to know and connect with you.

## Podcast

Podcasts are a terrific way to reach potential readers and build your brand. You can host your own podcast or be a guest on a popular podcast (or both!). I am an avid listener of podcasts, often listening while going for a walk, a run, or doing the laundry. I've found it to be an excellent way to connect with great minds and to learn from other's experiences. If you think you might enjoy this medium, give it a try. As with anything, if you decide to host a podcast, be professional and stick to a consistent schedule. Publish a new podcast once a week (e.g., every Monday). Let listeners know what to expect. Keep your podcasts focused on a topic (i.e. motivation). Keep podcasts at similar running times (e.g., 30 minutes). Publish show notes (transcription from your podcast) on your website. And before you begin your own podcast, be sure to listen faithfully to several others as you learn the ropes of what makes a podcast successful.

## Strong Bio

Keep your author bio and about page up to date. Be personal, but careful not to overshare. Open with an intriguing first sentence. Are you a bestselling author?

Awesome. Share that. Readers want to know. For example: *(Your name here) is a bestselling author and award-winning writer.* Let your readers know what kind of books you write (e.g., happily-ever-after love stories). Share your story in a few sentences. This is your opportunity to showcase your personality and your writing credentials. You may want to include a short, powerful review from readers. Provide a link to view/purchase your books. Also include an option to sign-up for your newsletter.

Professional bios should be brief. No one wants to read a three-page bio. We want to be entertained. We want to see your personality through your use of words (as a writer, you work magic with words every day!). We want to know your credentials, and we want to know a little bit about you. As an example, my current bio reads as follows (followed by links to my books and an option to sign up for my monthly newsletter):

Stacey Ritz is a bestselling author and award-winning writer. An empathetic and compassionate storyteller, Ritz wrote for a plethora of local and national news outlets, magazines, blogs, and websites (copywriter), prior to becoming a novelist. Her book, *Covered in Pet Fur* has gained attention from

RIVA Media and Animal Planet. She is the Executive Director and co-founder of Advocates 4 Animals, Inc. – a 501(c)3 non-profit animal welfare organization that has saved more than 11,000 lives (and counting). She currently resides in Ohio. Ritz is published through Rockville Publishing. You can interact with Stacey online via Stacey's Book Blog, on Pinterest, and Instagram.

Ritz writes the following genres:

*Nonfiction:*

*Motivation/Inspiration*

*Writing/Publishing*

*Animal Welfare*

*Fiction:*

*Love Stories*

## Professional Author Photo

Not only should you have a professional headshot as an author, it is also important to use the same headshot in all areas (e.g., website, back of the book, book distributors pages). Having spent years as a professional photographer, I cannot overestimate the importance of a good author photo. What constitutes a good author photo?

- Proper lighting (make sure the photo is not too dark).

- Engaging pose (look alive!).

- Background (if a background is too busy, it will detract from the author photo).

- Clothing (solid colors generally work best. Patterns tend to be too busy).

- Smile (engage with your fans with a natural smile).

- Ask your photographer for a hi-resolution, fully edited digital photograph (it's even better if you have the headshot in both color and black and white).

- Readers will judge you, and your books on your headshot (know what your headshot says about you. Does it say: friendly and welcoming?).

- Keep in mind, a poor author photo will signal "amateur" to potential readers. Your author photo speaks to readers, be sure your photo says what you want it to convey (e.g., engaging, upbeat).

## Word of Mouth

It may sound old fashioned, but it still works. I love eBook's (I can carry around hundreds of books on one device!), but I sometimes miss seeing faces hidden behind book covers (e.g., at the hair salon or the park). When paperbacks were more popular than eBooks, if I saw a book cover that looked interesting, I'd jot a note and search for the book. Now, of course, times have changed. I'm not spying on paperback covers, as most people are looking at a screen on their phone or device and I have no idea if they're reading an email, a text message, or a good book. Nevertheless, word of mouth marketing is not dead. If I'm having dinner with someone and they say, "I just finished reading the most amazing book", even if it's not in one of my typical reading genres, I can't help but perk up. If they make a compelling statement in favor of the book, I'm likely to give it a try.

While we can't control if, who, or when others will share our book title (or our author name) with other potential readers, we can ask our friends, family, and beta-readers to help us spread the word to each of their circles. In many cases, this tactic can prove incredibly beneficial. If you have ten beta-readers and they all share the book with their social circles (not only social media, but live, in person with their co-workers, friends, family), and if you have ten friends who do the same, and five family members...that adds up to a lot of additional potential readers who might buy and enjoy *your* book! Yes, it can be uncomfortable to ask others to spread the word about your book. However, if they've expressed enjoyment in reading your book, they will likely be happy to help you in this way. Don't be afraid to ask (and never underestimate the potential of this free marketing tool)!

## Brand Yourself

As a nonfiction writer, what is your expertise? Branding yourself as an expert is important. Think about it from a reader's perspective. Would you rather read a book on hiking from someone who has hiked thousands of miles around the globe, or from someone who *hopes* to hike one day? Likely you would choose to read the book written by the expert. We want to learn from those who are experienced. We want to know *how to*, we want to hear their stories, experiences, failures, successes, and to learn from their lessons. How do you brand yourself as an author? There are plenty of ways (and it is an ongoing process). Here are a few examples: speaking engagements, podcasts (host your own or contribute as a guest to others within your field of expertise), writing opinion pieces and freelance articles for news sources and magazines, and genuinely being excited (and knowledgeable) about what you do.

As a fiction author, you can brand yourself too, and it's important you do. How? By writing in the same genre. Once you've written several books (e.g., love stories), readers will begin knowing and trusting you within the genre. While branding yourself as an author (in a specific topic/genre) is not a direct marketing effort, it is essential to your long-term success as a writer. When readers know you are a "go-to" author for gripping thrillers, or for all things animal welfare, they will be more likely to remember your name and recommend you to others.

## Book Clubs

Visit with book clubs via video chat (e.g., Skype) or live in-person. Get creative! Consider providing free copies of your book to a book club, along with discussion questions. If book club members enjoy your book, they will be likely to spread the word to their circle of friends, family, and co-workers (as well as share on social media). They will also be likely to leave a positive online review and buy your next book. Don't overlook book clubs as a marketing tool (and don't limit yourself to only local clubs. With the power of technology, visiting is possible via video in many places).

## Local Bookstores

While many avid readers find their books online, there are still readers who prefer their local bookstore. Be creative when working with local bookstores. Ask to do a book signing and/or a reading from your book. Offer to raffle a free giveaway of your latest book. Bookstore customers can fill out their name and email address and drop it in a jar. Email everyone on a specific date with the winner's name(s) and mail an autographed copy or, better yet, meet them at the bookstore for pick-up.

## Collaboration

Working with other authors can be enjoyable and beneficial for our books. Again, this is an area where you can be creative. Create a Power Pack. If you and two other authors write in the same genre (e.g., motivational books), pair your books together. Offer your total of three books (on the same topic) at one price. For that one price, readers get three books from three different authors on a topic they enjoy. Even better? If a reader knows one of the three authors names, they are likely to purchase the Power Pack and read two authors new to them (this can create new readers for your other books!).

## Cross Promote

Do not view other books in your genre as competition. Rather, view them as friends. When we cross promote each other's work, especially when we write in the same genre (because we are likely to have many of the same readers), we can reach a wider array of readers. Cross promoting means sharing other authors book titles on your social media pages (not just your own). Share a book you've just read and loved. If the book is in a genre you write, your readers will appreciate the recommendation. The writing life is filled with hard work and long hours. Let's spend time lifting each other up and celebrating great works by other writers. As authors, we understand how much of our heart and soul we pour into our work. We understand that the creation of a published book is a labor of love as much as it is a daunting, grueling challenge. When we enjoy other authors creative works, let's share them with our own readers. Not only will your fans appreciate the recommendation, they will likely return the favor by recommending your books. As with other marketing options we've discussed in this chapter, cross promoting is not a direct marketing tool. However, it does help build your brand. It helps build your trust and credibility as an established author, too. Although we will likely never know an exact amount of readers who find their way to our books through this tool, it is always a good practice for professional.

## Build a Tribe

What is a tribe, or rather, *who* is *your* tribe? Seth Godin's book, *Tribes: We Need You to Lead Us* explains tribes as being human nature in occurrence. Tribes are groups of people who enjoy or are interested in a similar topic. Tribes can be religious, political, musical, etc. How can you build a tribe as an author? Slowly, but surely. But how, exactly? Build a tribe by doing what you love and sharing that thing with others. A tribe is like-minded people coming together to discuss that like-minded thing. There isn't a formula to create a tribe, rather it is more of a vision. Tribes evolve as a leader evolves and as an author, you can be that leader. If you write nonfiction in your area of expertise of health and nutrition, you can create a tribe by: writing more books in your genre, having a professional website with helpful articles and information, speaking at events, hosting a podcast, writing a blog, etc. In a sense, building a tribe is a culmination of every marketing and branding effort you make on your books behalf.

## Covers Matter

Unless you are a graphic designer, creating a D.I.Y. (do-it-yourself) cover for your book can spell disaster. Your book cover is your first impression to a potential reader. Make it a good one! Yes, it costs money to hire a cover designer, but the cost of a professional cover is well worth it. I created a D.I.Y. (do-it-yourself) cover for my first indie published book. I had a strong brand (built up over more than a decade) and sales were fairly strong for the first several months (with most sales coming directly from supporters of my brand). However, after a while, sales slowed. And I realized I wasn't thrilled with my cover. The cover was eventually updated to a professional design and sales rose (this time, not from my direct supporters, but from readers stumbling across my book and noticing it because of the new and much improved cover).

As a book blogger, my inbox is filled with book review requests every week. When I am considering reading a book for review, I look at its cover. I know instantly if the cover is professionally done or D.I.Y. And in all honesty, I am drawn to the professional covers. A professional cover tells readers that the author takes their work seriously and that they want to put their best work out into the world. I totally understand the cost issue on book covers. But the cost a professional design will save you (in loss of readers— meaning those who will avoid your book because of a poor cover) and the additional cost it will earn you (a professional design will attract more readers to your book) are well worth it. Remember, in jump starting your writing life, you want to create a sustainable long-term income from your writing. A well designed, professional book cover is a helpful way to do that. Books are judged (and often in a matter of a few short seconds) by:

- The appeal of their cover

- Title and tag-line

- Author recognition

- Reviews

Before working with a professional cover designer (there are both companies and individuals who offer these services), study book covers in your genre. Look for commonalities in the covers. The commonalities are what draw the readers of that particular genre to the book (i.e. love stories have colors that are light and airy, among many other commonalities). Be sure to let your designer know to include these elements in your cover. It's always best if you can find a designer who has experience creating covers in your genre. The bottom line is, hire a professional (for book covers, editing and formatting. Presentation matters!) You are a professional in the field of writing. Let the professionals in the field of design assist you in making your book the best it can be.

## Purchase Ads

Purchasing advertisement spots on social media (e.g.,

Facebook) or mediums such as Book Bub can be highly beneficial to short term book sales. If strategized properly (with staggered ads throughout the year), purchased ads can increase the revenue from your books long-term. However, remember marketing should not be a one-time effort (a one-time effort will produce a one-time, short-term result), it is an ongoing one. Similar to the cost and effort of a professional book cover design, the cost may seem steep up front, however, the results are often beneficial, much outweighing the cost. Keep in mind, regardless of how much money and time you spend on marketing efforts, if you haven't written a compelling story, no amount of marketing will create long term sustainable income from your product.

## Samples

Include a free sample (e.g., first chapter) of another book you've written at the end of your book (this is most beneficial when the free sample included is within the same genre of the book the reader has just completed). A free sample, also referred to as a "teaser" has hooked me to a new book many times. If I've just finished reading an enjoyable book, and I read a compelling sample of another book by the same author, I put my trust in them and purchase the book. There are thousands upon thousands of books to choose from in any genre. If I've found an author I like and trust, it makes it easy to purchase their next book when I've just read an enjoyable free sample (and if I'm reading an eBook, which I likely am, I only have to click one button at the end of the sample, to be taken to the purchase page. And then, voila! The book is on my device, ready for reading at that moment. Writing really is magic!).

## Merchandise

With the rise of print-on-demand, creating merchandise is another way to create revenue for your writing life. *Merchandise? But I thought we were writers who create stories, which become books?* I see you raising your eyebrows and asking this question right now. Merchandise such as mugs, T-shirts, companion workbooks (for nonfiction books), etc. can be another way to market your books. If you write love stories, you can create mugs with a beautiful quote from your book. The mug can also include your book title and a link to your website (side note: when using print-on-demand services, always check the quality of products first). You may find new potential readers through sales of your merchandise. You may also build your author brand by offering such products to your growing number of fans. It's another way for fans to remember your name, your book, and to recommend you to their circle of friends, family, and co-workers (and if you utilize print-on-demand services, there is no out of pocket cost—only what it costs you in time to design the items, and the minimal cost of ordering each item to check quality before offering them for sale to your fans).

## Videos

YouTube is a terrific medium to reach potential readers. Authors can read the first chapter of their book. Offer a book trailer (much like a movie trailer) to entice readers to buy your book. You can also utilize videos on your website and to post to social media. Author interviews (with you!) speaking, not necessarily about your book, but on topic, can generate new interest in your book as well. Just because we're writers (and often introverts) doesn't mean we have to stay hidden behind our keyboards. We can let ourselves be seen and offer another way for readers to find and learn more about us and our brand.

## On Sale!

Don't be afraid of trial and error when it comes to marketing your book (after all, this is how you will learn what combination of ongoing marketing efforts work best for your work). As the entrepreneur of your writing life, realizing the importance of sales will increase *your* sales! The key to creating sales is to create urgency (e.g., this price is offered for one day only!). Outside of offering a standard sale on your book (e.g., a lowered price for a specific short amount of time), don't forget to be innovative. Creating urgency and offering a free digital bonus product can create a profitable impact on book sales. For example, create an offer such as the following:

*$2.99 Sale! Tuesday Only! Buy the book today and get access to an exclusive audio interview with the author. Offer valid Tuesday only!*

Another idea, if you've written a book series, you can offer the first book in the series for free or for a discounted price of $0.99 (once the whole series is available). Readers will be more likely to pick up your book for free (or for a minimal cost) and if they like it, they will become a fan and purchase the remaining books in the series.

Free book giveaways are another form of sale that can bring new readers (e.g., offer free giveaways via your e-newsletter list, or on websites such as bookfunnel.com and similar sites). Experiment with book sales and giveaways and find what works best for your books. While you may shy away from offering a sale, the amount of revenue you will make per book during the sale period will drastically decrease. Keep in mind that you can find new readers through this method. And by finding new readers who enjoy your books, you will increase your future book sales.

## THE REAL DEAL

Readers are not likely to remember your name until they've read (and enjoyed) four or more of your books (typically books written in the same genre). While not likely to remember book titles, readers will, in time, remember your name. Your name is your brand (e.g., many people say they need a

Kleenex, when in fact the product is a tissue. Kleenex is the brand name. In the book world, readers know the names Danielle Steele, Nicholas Sparks, etc.). Knowing this, I encourage you to continue writing books in your genre. The bigger your backlist, the more likely you will be to attract readers to your books. In a discussion of writing more books within your genre, Kristine Kathryn Rusch, author of *Closing the Deal...On Your Terms: Agents, Contracts, and Other Considerations* explained: "Your one intellectual property (e.g., book) is like a house. If you leverage your copyright, you can turn it into a subdivision" (note: this is a must-read book for all authors if you wish to save money and maximize your earnings).[1]

How will you drive your own traffic (i.e., book sales)? How will you drive traffic to your website? To get your books in libraries? The answer is: start with one. Start with one reader (outside of your circle of family and friends). Then grow. Build a relationship with your fans. This is generally a slow process and one where it is beneficial to be the tortoise rather than the hare. Build that relationship through building trust. How do you build trust? With a professional product (i.e., well-told story, edited, appealing book cover, formatting and design, website, etc.). Let readers know you'll deliver a compelling story every time. Let them know they can depend on you for good content (in your specific genre or topic of expertise). It can be overwhelming. Start with one reader. One newsletter subscriber. One Instagram fan. One online review. It is a start. One reader is a start that will take you to two. And then five, ten, fifty, one-hundred, and so on. It all starts with one. Do not be discouraged when you have one reader. Instead, celebrate. You have a reader! You are, after all, jump starting your writing life and you're in this for the long haul. Looking at the big picture, realize you are running a marathon, not a sprint.

Marketing is an essential part of an author's life, regardless of how you choose to publish. Without marketing, your book is not likely to sell. There are many ways to market your book and it is up to you to find the right combination for your author business. Some marketing is free (outside of the price of your time). There are also low-cost marketing options and those that come at a premium. Study the market. Make strategic decisions based on your long-term goals. And find what works best for you. Marketing often means taking a risk and utilizing trial and error.

It is a myth to do marketing once and forget about it. It's unrealistic to publish your book, and neglect it by forgetting to advertise. Although the specific marketing will differ for every author, one thing that will always remain the same is that it requires an ongoing effort. Is marketing hard? Yes. But remember, you are jump starting your writing career. You are working to create a sustainable long-term income. You want to create a sustainable long-term model when it comes to marketing your books.

## 10

Building Your Community

*"If you want to be a writer you must do two things above all others: read a lot, and write a lot."*

*-Stephen King*

"Tree roots are connected and are scientifically documented as sending carbon to each other (helping). They cooperate, not compete with each other. They send messages back and forth to share resources with each other. If one tree has a lot of water and another nearby tree is sick, they'll send water to them via the root system. Trees are super cooperatives" shared NPR's Ted Radio Hour.[1]

Mother trees (also known as "hub trees") are larger and will help seedlings in their area. They also reduce the spread of their own roots and make room for their "kids…Trees need a diverse community to thrive, just as we do. Trees share resources with neighbors to help everyone be more vibrant and healthy." We can do the same. When we realize we need each other, we can all thrive and be at our best. We all have a role to play, just as trees do in their communities. It's when we all play our role, to the best of our best abilities, that we all succeed.

Why am I talking about trees? Yes, I realize this is a book on writing (not trees!). But, as writers, we can learn a lot from trees. Like trees, we are a community. As writers, we can work together with others in our community to create our best products (e.g., professional editors, cover designers, formatters, beta-readers, proofreaders, marketing professionals, and of course, our readers!). It would be boring if we were all the same. Luckily, we're not. And because of that, we can work together, each utilizing our own strengths and talents to contribute to the whole. Trees cooperate with each other because they understand there is enough goodness for everyone. We can do the same. There is not a limited well of success to pull from. Rather, the well is limitless. Not only can we collaborate with other professionals and work to earn the trust and loyalty of our readers, we can also support our fellow writers. If we read a book we enjoy, we can post a kind online review to help other readers find the book. We can share other author's books we've enjoyed on our social media pages. We can co-write a book with another author. We can invite other authors in our genre to be a guest blogger on our website. We can create a Power Pack of three or four books with authors who have written similar books to ours (and work together to reach more readers). We can offer to beta-read another authors work. We can be active members of the writing and reading community. We can volunteer for events such as NEA's Read Across America to promote the joy of reading. We can mentor or tutor young and aspiring writers (if you haven't read *True Notebooks* by Mark Salzman, I highly recommend this book). We can join a local writing group, attend seminars, retreats, and workshops. We can build our e-mail lists to connect with readers. We can become members of writing associations based on our genre (e.g., Cat Writers Association), aligning ourselves with other professionals in the field. And we can keep doing what we do: writing.

While there are many people who dream of

publishing a book, many never do. Many others stop after just two or three books. Why? Because it's hard. The writing life takes a lot of work and provides no guarantees. Some books publish, never selling 100 copies. That being said, one of the most important things you can do when jump starting your writing career (whether you're just starting or reigniting) is to define your definition of success. Decide what you want from your writing life and why you're doing it. What is your definition of success? Likely, no two writers will have the same answer. If your definition of success is to publish one book or fifty, great. If your definition of success is to sell 1000 or 100,000 copies of your published book, awesome. Or maybe your definition of success is to be a bestselling author. Decide what your definition is, write it down, and post it in your writing space (somewhere you will see it every day).

Susan Cain, author of *Quiet: The Power of Introverts in a World that Can't Stop Talking*, articulately explains the pain of face-to-face networking for introverts (many writers are introverts, yours truly included). She writes about how one new meaningful relationship can be more powerful than a handful of business cards (cards of people you can't even remember). This is an important point to keep in mind when building our communities. Think quality, not quantity. When we build quality relationships based on mutual trust and respect, we build lasting relationships. We build connections. We enjoy our work. We grow and flourish. We become our best selves. And like the trees, we build thriving communities.

# 11

# Coping with Self-Doubt

*"I think new writers are too worried that it has all been said before. Sure it has, but not by you."*

-*Asha Dornfest*

The words LISTEN and SILENT are spelled with the same six letters. Stop and think about that for a moment. And then pause and listen to your inner voice (aka your gut, your intuition). The previous chapter prompted the question: what does success mean *to you*? Be silent and listen to that inner voice. Once you've got your answer (and likely, this will change as you grow and evolve), answer the next question: do you ever face self-doubt? If you said yes, you're in good company. We all do, writers and non-writers alike. Self-doubt is natural. It's normal. It's to be expected. Therefore, the real question becomes, as writers how do we cope with self-doubt?

Often, unpublished writers fear rejection and failure. Published writers fear poor reviews and a lack of sales. We are all guilty of falling victim to the "I'll be happy when..." syndrome. It's when we tell ourselves (whether out loud or in our own heads) I'll be happy when... (fill in the blank. For example, I'll be happy when my book is published. Or, I'll be happy once my book has ten five-star reviews. Or, I'll be happy when my book becomes a movie. The I'll be happy when... syndrome can strike at any time. And unless we take time to pay attention and catch ourselves in the act, we will fall victim to its crippling self-doubt every time. Next time you catch yourself saying "I'll be happy when..." stop. Change the statement. Try something along the lines of: "Right now, I'm grateful for..." Change your focus from self-doubt and worry, to appreciation for the good things in your life at this very moment. Often, this technique can keep self-doubt at bay.

Self-doubt doesn't only come from the "I'll be happy when..." syndrome. It can creep up on us from any number of things. Self-doubt, put simply, is when we worry that we are not good enough. It's coming to terms with vulnerability. And as writers, vulnerability is part of the career. Self-doubt can be stirred up from a need for validation, something many writers fall victim to. We want our editors to tell us our story is fabulous and we have minimal edits. We want our beta-readers to assure us our novel will be a bestseller. We want our readers to enjoy our books and to post five-star reviews and recommend our book to their friends. We want to know we are enough. We long for validation as we worry that we're a fraud. Self-doubt is often called "imposter syndrome", and you can see why. With a lack of feedback, we worry our *work* isn't good (and often translate that even further into "*we* are not good"). With feedback, we worry that we're not as good as those giving the feedback say we are. The bottom line is, we worry. It's true, some worry can serve us well (e.g., urging us to do our best work), but excessive worry does just the opposite. Excessive worry can kill creativity and plague our mind with nagging thoughts.

The fear of judgement or criticism, the fear of rejection or failure; they carry with them the burden of self-doubt. Perfectionism can be paralyzing. After all, who is to say when our work is perfect? What is perfect, anyway? Perfect is an ideal that doesn't exist. And if it doesn't exist, why do we let it bring us so much self-doubt? As writers, if we do our best work, if we work with other professionals to create the best product (book) we can, we can stand tall and be proud of that fact. Does this assure us that we'll never receive anything less than a 4-star review? No. Does this path promise us our book will sell well? No. Does it guarantee us that no one will ever say a negative word about us or our work? No. You get the point. We can do the work, but there is no security in the fact that we will be free of judgement, criticism, rejection, and failure. All we can do is do our best. Collaborate with other professionals. Find ways to reach our readers. Turn our readers into fans. And keep doing what we do. Keep writing, because we're writers.

Speaking of judgement and criticism, what about our inner critic? Negative self-talk is something we've all dealt with at one time or another. You know that little voice that you hear after you've just finished the first draft of your novel. You feel so excited, so relieved to type "THE END", but then the inner critic surfaces. You wake up the next morning filled with doubt. *Is my book good enough? Will the story hold the readers interest? Should I toss it and start over? Oh no! I'm really going to let someone else read this at some point?* Negative self-talk can be debilitating.

And then there's good old comparitinitis (when we compare ourselves to others). We all do it at times. We publish our first book, yet find ourselves looking at bestselling authors who have twenty-five books under their belt, and we scold ourselves for having only sold a handful of copies. We see an author in our genre with 2,000 positive reviews, and realize our book only has 2. Comparitinitis makes us feel bad. It feeds self-doubt. It's interesting to know what other writers are doing and what they've accomplished, but they are not us and we are not them. Your superpower is being uniquely you. Use it. Be you. And stop comparing. Be interested in other writer's work, yes. But don't compare. Just be you and keep writing.

Working toward a goal is hard work. It's also important that we understand that working toward a goal is not always going to be fun. When we are dedicated to our writing, when we declare *our* unique definition of success, and when we when we set specific and measurable goals, the compound effect takes place. The compound effect is when the compilation of our ongoing hard work takes effect.

It's not something that happens overnight. It takes time. It takes patience. It takes believing in ourselves (despite the self-doubt that comes our way). The compound effect is when all of our (past and present) actions work together to reach our unique definition of success. This can only be possible when we keep working. When we work through the hard times. When we find pockets of time to write on days when we think there is no time. When we write even when we experience crippling self-doubt. When we keep working toward our goal, even when some days feel boring. Regardless of the method in which self-doubt finds us, when we overcome it we can turn doubt into "do".

## DOUBT

If self-doubt is inevitable, how can we overcome it? Use the following methods to cope with self-doubt. Keep in mind, it is not a one-and-done solution. Self-doubt has no restraints. It can strike at any moment and for any length of time, if you give it permission to do so. Each time it arrives, try using one or more of the following solutions (it may require a different combination each time. Find what works best for you).

- Believe in yourself.

- Create healthy writing habits.

- Think long-term.

- Do not fall victim to comparitinitis.

- Change "I'll be happy when…" statements into, "Right now I'm grateful for…"

- Introduce yourself as a writer. Celebrate the fact that you are a storyteller.

- Write every day.

- Define your definition of success. Set specific and measurable goals.

- Learn to be okay with vulnerability.

- Build your community (of writers, collaborators, and readers). Find your tribe.

- Build a newsletter/email list.

- Find your path.

- Be a constant reader (always be learning and growing).

- Trust your unique path as a writer.

- Find your voice.

- Be persistent.

- Be a professional.

- Develop professional relationships (e.g., cover designer, editors).

- Learn and embrace the business side of authorship (you are the entrepreneur of your writing life).

- Set deadlines and stick to them.

- Stay motivated.

- Read other authors articles, blogs, and books.

- Read quotes and poems.

- Participate in different writing projects (e.g., non-profit newsletters, magazines, blogs, co-write, etc.).

- Attend seminars, workshops, conferences.

- Celebrate other writers' successes.

- Don't quit when you're worried. Learn to take a breather and then get back to work.

- Remind yourself that writing is not about fame and fortune, it's about loving the work you do and wanting to make the world a brighter, better place. It's about connecting.

- Learn from reviews (5-star and 1-star) on other books written in your genre.

- Celebrate each step you climb (don't ignore the many little things that happen as you continue to grow).

- If you receive a poor review, remind yourself that it is only one person's opinion.

- Keep a journal: write down all of the positive reviews you receive on your book. If you're having a bad day or just need a bit of inspiration, revisit the comments in the journal.

- Keep writing!

In her book *Daring Greatly: How the Courage to be Vulnerable Transforms the Way we Live, Love, Parent, and Lead*, researcher and author and Brené Brown shares Theodore Roosevelt's quote, pointing out how it relates to the courage to be vulnerable. I read this often, as a reminder to keep doing what I'm doing. To keep writing. To keep going. This quote applies strongly to us, as writers (e.g., editing, reviews, feedback).

"It is not the critic who counts; not the man who points out how the strong man stumbles, or where the doer of deeds could have done them better. The credit belongs to the man who is actually in the arena, whose face is marred by dust and sweat and blood; who strives valiantly; who errs, who comes short again and again, because there is no effort without error and shortcoming; but who does actually strive to do the deeds; who knows great enthusiasms, the great devotions; who spends himself in a worthy cause; who at the best knows in the end the triumph of high achievement, and who at the worst, if he fails, at least fails while daring greatly, so that his place shall never be with those cold and timid souls who neither know victory nor defeat."

Are you daring greatly in your life? With your writing? When is the last time you felt truly vulnerable in your writing life? When was the last time you experienced self-doubt? How did you overcome it?

Are you overwhelmed yet? It is absolutely okay to feel this way. Writing can be staggering at times. Between deadlines, editors, formatting, reviews, schedules, and warding off self-doubt, there is a lot to juggle, in addition to the sting of vulnerability. But you can do it. Learn from every failure. Yes, there is risk involved in the writing life. Keep learning. Keep writing. Keep working. Keep doing your thing. And always remember that you have a rare angle. You have a unique voice. Use it. When I co-wrote our bestseller, *Covered in Pet Fur: How to Start an Animal Rescue, The Right Way*, we knew there were other books on the topic. Yet, we still wrote the book. We had a unique angle. As the co-founders of an animal welfare organization, we wanted to share what we'd learned, in hopes of helping others save the lives of additional homeless, abused, and neglected animals. And we've found the book is doing just that. We receive frequent e-mails, letters, and feedback letting us know how much the book has been an asset to others. And we are delighted. Our hearts are warmed. Our experiences combined with our words are serving to help other people and save the lives of animals around the globe. As an author and animal advocate, it's a wonderful feeling. Use your voice.

Use your experiences. Write your story and share it with the world. We're waiting to hear it.

# 12

---

# Get to Work

*"If there is a book that you want to read but it hasn't been written yet, then you must write it."*

*-Toni Morrison*

What path will you blaze? What stories will you write? What are your goals? What conferences will you attend this year? What writing groups will you join? Will you mentor or tutor a child who dreams of being a writer? Where will you find small pockets of time to write on your busiest days? What is your first small step? Do you want be published in a literary magazine? A newspaper? Blog? Do you want to be a speaker? What books are on your nightstand (or waiting on your eReader) to be read? Do you have an attitude of gratitude? I read somewhere that the most important decision you'll ever make is the one to be happy. I say this to myself every single day. Life throws curveballs at all of us. Things can be tough. But when I remember this saying, to make the decision to be happy, it changes everything for me. Are you happy? If not, can you make the decision to be happy right now?

Speaking of goals, have you written yours down? Do you spend time visualizing success (your unique definition of it) for yourself? Do you write every day? Do you read every day? Actor Jim Carrey, while not a writer he is a creative, practiced the power of visualization when he was broke and poor. He said he did it because it "made him feel better." As a guest on *The Oprah Show*[1] Carrey explained how he would sit in his car and visualize having directors interested in him. He wrote a check to himself for ten million dollars, for acting services rendered. He dated the check three years into the future (on Thanksgiving Day). He placed the check in his wallet where it grew faded and worn. He continued to visualize good things for himself. He continued to work hard and stayed focused on his goal. Just before the date written on his check, he was given ten million dollars for his role in the movie *Dumb and Dumber*. After hearing Carrey tell this story, Oprah explained, "Visualization works for you if you work hard." Are you working hard?

> *"Writing Is hard. That's why so few people stick to it and actually finish things. And why you have a right to be immensely proud when you finish something."*
>
> *-Andy Ihnatko*

Submerse yourself in your passion. I'm assuming if you've read this far, you have a passion for writing. Give up bad habits (e.g., too much social media) and pick up good ones (e.g., more reading and writing). Set your priorities. Make time for what really matters to you; whether it's writing or any endeavor, person, pet, etc. Make time because the time is now. Don't say, "tomorrow I will…". Don't say anything (if you want to say it, *write it*). Do the work that is important and meaningful to you. Tell the stories that are inside of you.

The hardest part is starting. Whether you're just starting your writing journey, you've stepped away to take a breather for a bit and you're ready to jump back in, or you're currently writing a bestseller, take a deep breath and begin. Keep working. Keep writing. Every. Single. Day. As Nelson Mandela famously said: "*It always seems impossible until it's done.*" When self-doubt strikes, overcome it utilizing a combination of self-empowering techniques. And remember the quote above. Remember that you are surrounded by a community of writers who understand. Remember that your fans (or future fans) are waiting on your book. Yours may be the one to change their life. You never know.

> "*If I had asked people what they wanted, they would have said faster horses.*"

> *-Henry Ford*

Who are your favorite authors (and why)? What are your favorite books (and why)? Make lists with your answers. Study the reasons and emulate them (*your* reasons, not the work of others) in your own work. When it comes to motivation, a few of my favorite books include:

- *The Power of Habit: Why We Do What We Do In Life And Business* (Charles Duhigg)
- *The Alchemist* (Paulo Coelho)

- *Who Moved My Cheese* (Spencer Johnson)

- *If You Don't Have Big Breasts Put Ribbons On Your Pigtails: And Other Lessons I Learned From My Mom (Barbara Corcoran)*

- *Still Writing: The Perils and Pleasures of a Creative Life (Dani Shapiro)*

- *Tiny Beautiful Things: Advice on Love and Life from Dear Sugar (Cheryl Strayed)*

When it's time to share your own books with the world, realize that your books won't be for everyone. That doesn't mean they're not good enough. If you do the work and stay true to yourself, the right audience will find their way to you. Always welcome feedback and constructive criticism, especially from your beta-readers, editors, proofreaders and all of your readers. It's not the easiest thing to do, but it will help you become a stronger writer and a more compelling storyteller.

*"Trust that all you've learned was worth learning, no matter what answer you have or do not have about what practical use it has in your life. Let whatever mysterious*

*starlight that guided you this far guide you onward into the crazy beauty that awaits."*

*-Cheryl Strayed, Brave Enough*

Never forget that you are the C.E.O. of your writing life. You are the entrepreneur of your writing career. Build your author business so that it will support the lifestyle you want. Create a writing life that allows you to work hard and reach your definition of success.

As a book blogger, I not only write book reviews, I also interview authors (and share those interview sessions on my blog *StaceyRitzBooks.com*). I love meeting other authors and learning what inspires them and how they got started on their writing journey. I am fascinated by our interviews. One of my favorite questions to ask authors is *when* they knew they wanted to be a writer. I share a few of these answers, from several talented authors, with you now. When I asked author, comedian, actor, improvisor, and producer Marcel St. Pierre to share when he knew he wanted to be a writer, he explained:

*"Seriously forever. There's a photo my mom has of me at about 9 or 10 years old, hunched over a scribbler (the*

*Canadian word for notebook) over the kitchen table, writing a story with a pen. It's just always something I've done. I was the one kid in class who would always go "YAY" when the other kids would moan and gripe when the teacher told us our assignment was creative writing. I was always a bookworm, from the moment I learned to read, even before going to school. I was always holding on to comic books, story books, any books at all. I had this great babysitter who encouraged me by having me write stories based on our favourite T.V. shows, and she'd write some for me, too. I still have her handwritten, loose-leaf stories in storage. I'm a bit of a sentimentalist that way. Case in point, maybe a dozen years ago, I went back to my home town and found a box at a yard sale that had a copy of every single language arts reader I'd ever had back in grade school in the 70s. Needless to say I bought the box."*

Author Gail Olmsted shared her experience:

*"My oldest friend Laurie swears that I used to say that I wanted to write a book back in my early teens. I thought about [my book] Jeep Tour and pictured the story for several years in my mind, before I actually started putting*

*pen to paper. Once I got started, I never stopped. Now I'm working on my 4th book!"*

Sean Paul-Thomas, author of *The Old Man and the Princess*, shared his thoughts on the topic of knowing when he wanted to become a writer:

*"When I was around 12 or 13 I watched Bram Stokers Dracula for the very first time. I fell in love with the movie and suddenly became inspired to write a sequel, in novel form. So I did (lol) And it was awful ? But then a few months later I decided to write something else, something from my own imagination, and it was a little less awful. So I just kept on going."*

Author Robert Skuce said he always knew he wanted to be a writer, explaining:

*"I think I have always wanted to be a writer. It just took me a long time to get the courage to chase that dream."*

While writer Michelle Sommers shared:

*"I don't think it was a conscious decision at first. I've always just written. When I was younger I tended more*

*toward poems and short stories. And never for anyone's eyes but my own. The desire to write something mainstream came in my twenties. But I never followed it. At that stage in my life, my confidence was sadly lacking. And there was always that niggling self-doubt – what if I fail? It took another twenty years for me to find the courage, sit down at my keyboard and just write. And I've been writing ever since."*

Now it's your turn. When did *you* know you wanted to be a writer?

**"The difference between who you are and who you want to be is what you do."**

Dare to be great. Dare to try. Dare to dedicate yourself to your passion. Sacrifice is required to obtain any goal. Put in your 10,000 hours and enjoy the journey. You never know where it will lead you. Be open to opportunities and experiences. And keep writing, because you are a writer. It's what we do.

Whether you have fiction or nonfiction ready to be written and inside of you, if you feel the story, if you've logged your hours and you're ready, write your book. Your first draft will be rough, it will contain plenty of edits and re-writes, but you'll *have* something to edit. You'll have *your* beautiful manuscript in your hands.

So, go ahead. What are you waiting for? Jump start your writing career right now. Don't put it off until tomorrow. Do it now. Your story is inside of you, ready to be told. It's time. You can do this.

**Write *your* story.**

# BIBLIOGRAPHY

**Prologue**

[1] ABC News, *The Impact of To Kill a Mockingbird*, http://abcnews.go.com/US/harper-lee-impact-kill-mockingbird/story?id=37055512, February 19, 2016. Accessed January 20, 2017.

[2] Open Education Database, *50 Books that Changed the World*, http://oedb.org/ilibrarian/50_books_that_changed_the_world/, January 26, 2010. Accessed February 1, 2017.

**Chapter 1**

[1] Hutchinson, Bryan. (2015), *The Audacity to be a Writer: 50 Inspiring Articles on Writing that Could Change Your Life*, CreateSpace Independent Publishing Platform.

[2] Ritz, Stacey. (2017), *Be Awesome: How to Live Your Best Life*, CreateSpace Independent Publishing Platform.

[3] Joanne G. Phillips, Author Mission Statements, https://joannegphillips.wordpress.com/2012/08/14/author-mission-statements/, August 14, 2012. Accessed January 7, 2017.

[4] Platt, Sean & Truant, Johnny. (2016), Iterate and Optimize: Optimize your Creative Business for Profit, Sterling & Stone.

[5] TEDx [TEDx Talks]. (2015, May 26). *How to Value People Over Profits | Dale Partridge | TEDxBend*

. Retrieved from https://www.youtube.com/watch?v=-o9mENH56I8

## Chapter 2

[1] Sound-Mind, *Positive Self Talk*, http://www.sound-mind.org/positive-self-talk.html#.WHU92FyQxPY, No Date. Accessed January 21, 2017.

[2] Forbes, *Surround Yourself with the Right People*, http://www.forbes.com/2010/08/20/work-friendship-negativity-forbes-woman-leadership-success.html, August 20, 2010. Accessed January 22, 2017.

[3] Writers Digest, *How Book Advances Work: A Simple Explanation for Writers*,

http://www.writersdigest.com/online-editor/how-book-advances-work-a-simple-explanation-for-writers, March 10, 2014. Accessed January 19, 2017.

[4] The Creative Penn, *Creating Intellectual Property Assets*

*Through Writing Can Change Your Life*, http://www.thecreativepenn.com/2012/04/12/ intellectual-property-assets/, April 12, 2012. Accessed January 10, 2017.

[5] Huffington Post, *How Two 15-Minute Walks Daily During Work Has Increased Company Productivity by 30%*, http://www.huffingtonpost.com/young-entrepreneur-council/how-two-15-minute-walks-d_b_7978520.html, August 17, 2016. Accessed January 9, 2017.

**Chapter 5**

[1] The Write Practice, *The Pros and Cons of Panters and Plotters*, http://thewritepractice.com/plotters-pantsers/, No Date. Accessed February 1, 2017.

2 The Creative Penn Podcast. "Writing Tips: Outlining For Genre And Literary Fiction With Libbie Hawker" Podcast Recording. http://www.thecreativepenn.com/ 2016/05/23/writing-outlining-libbie-hawker/, 2016, May 23.

[3] New York Book Editors, *Planning to Outline Your Novel? Don't*,

http://nybookeditors.com/2013/09/outlining/, No Date. Accessed February 5, 2017.

[4] Jerry Jenkins, *How to Outline a Novel (Even if You're Not an Outliner)*, http://www.jerryjenkins.com/how-

to-outline-a-novel/, October 5, 2015. Accessed February 7, 2017.

[5] The Creative Penn, *Outlining Your Novel: Why and How,* http://www.thecreativepenn.com/2010/01/25/outlining-novel/, January 25, 2010. Accessed January 16, 2017.

[6] Letter Pile, *How to Outline a Novel,* https://letterpile.com/writing/How-to-Outline-a-Novel, July 15, 2016. Accessed February 8, 2017.

## Chapter 6

[1] Writer Unboxed, *Review of James Pattersons Writing Masterclass,* http://writerunboxed.com/2015/07/13/review-of-james-pattersons-writing-masterclass/, July 13, 2015. Accessed February 1, 2017.

[2] TED Radio Hour [TED Radio Hour]. (2015, December 18). *The Hero's Journey | TED Radio Hour | TED Radio Hour*

. Retrieved from: https://www.youtube.com/watch?v=0nVoA0AjmTo.

[3] Archer, Jodie & Jockers, Matthew. (2016), *The Bestseller Code: Anatomy of the Blockbuster Novel,* St. Martin's Griffin.

[4] Write it Sideways, *How and When to Use White Space in Writing,*

https://writeitsideways.com/how-and-when-to-use-white-space-in-writing, March 15, 2011. Accessed February 1, 2017.

5 Authors Helping Writers Become Authors, *What's the Difference Between Conflict and Tension?*, http://www.helpingwritersbecomeauthors.com/ conflict-and-tension/, December 5, 2012. Accessed February 1, 2017.

6 The Write Practice, How to Unlock All Five Senses in Your Writing, http://thewritepractice.com/five-senses-in-writing, No Date. Accessed January 20, 2017.

7 Marie TV. "Elizabeth Gilbert & Marie Forleo on Fear, Authenticity and Big Magic" Online Video Clip. https://www.youtube.com/watch?v=HyUYa-BnjU8, 2015, September 22.

8 Write and Publish Like a Pro, *Three Reasons for Using a Pen Name*, http://www.smallbluedog.com/3-reasons-for-using-a-pen-name.html, No Date. Accessed February 2, 2017.

9 Mental Floss, *Authors Who Write Under Different Pen Names*, http://mentalfloss.com/uk/books/28108/10-authors-who-write-under-different-pen-names, No Date. Accessed January 20, 2017.

**Chapter 7**

[1] Jane Friedman, *A Definition of Author Platform*, https://janefriedman.com/author-platform-definition/, July 25, 2016. Accessed January 20, 2017.

[2] The Write Life, *Author Platform: Here's What All the Fuss is About*, https://thewritelife.com/author-platform/, May 21, 2014. Accessed January 12, 2017.

## Chapter 8

[1] Writers' Center: Eastern Washington University, *Active Vs. Passive Voice*, http://research.ewu.edu/c.php?g=425370&p=3010640, No Date. Accessed January 18, 2017.

[2] She's Novel, *Things Editors Wish Authors Knew*, https://www.shesnovel.com/blog/editors-wish-authors-knew, No Date. Accessed January 12, 2017.

[3] The Creative Penn, *Editing and The Writing Craft: Tips From an Editor,* http://www.thecreativepenn.com/2014/08/11/editing-writing-craft-tips/, August 11, 2014. Accessed January 10, 2017.

[4] The Creative Penn, *How to Find the Right Editor for Your Book and More Editing Questions Answered*, http://www.thecreativepenn.com/2014/07/14/how-to-find-the-right-editor/, July 14, 2014. Accessed January 19, 2017.

[5] Writer Beware, *Vetting an Independent Editor*, http://accrispin.blogspot.co.uk/2012/05/vetting-

independent–editor.html, May 3, 2012., Accessed January 5, 2017.

## Chapter 9

[1] Kristine Kathryn Rusch, *Business Musings*, http://kriswrites.com/, No Date. Accessed January 18, 2017.

## Chapter 10

[1] TED Radio Hour [TED Radio Hour]. (2017, January 13). *Networks | TED Radio Hour | TED Radio Hour* (video file). Retrieved from https://www.youtube.com/watch?v=7P5RbXC8_3k.

## Chapter 12

[1] Law of Attraction Tactics. "Jim Carrey Tells Oprah How He Visualized 10 Million Dollars" Online Video Clip. https://www.youtube.com/watch?v=DXwVD2ncqfE. 2014, Nov 25.

# ABOUT THE AUTHOR

Stacey Ritz is the bestselling author of *Covered in Pet Fur* (Rockville Publishing). She is the Executive Director and co-founder of Advocates 4 Animals, Inc., a 501(c)3 non-profit animal welfare organization that has saved more than 11,000 lives (and counting). Ritz writes both non-fiction and fiction. She lives in the Midwest with her family, including a handful of foster cats and dogs. Learn more at *www.*staceyritzbooks.com.